BUTTER SIZE OF A TURKEY EGG

Butter Size of a Turkey Egg:
The Foodways and Social World of the Ladies
of the
Presbyterian Church
of Kingston, Pennsylvania in 1907

Including Four-Hundred and Fifty
Of Their Everyday Recipes

By

Robert W. Surridge, D.Ed.

Published By
Luzerne County Historical Society

Acknowledgements

I would like to thank the following individuals for making this book possible: Beverly Jones for proofreading and editing; Amanda Fontenova and Anthony Brooks from the Luzerne County Historical Society for their assistance and encouragement; and Professor Michael Barton for his thoughtful comments, corrections and suggestions. A special thank you to my wife, Carole, for her ongoing support, encouragement and guidance.

Manufactured in the United States of America.

ISBN-13: 978-0985339913 Luzerne County Historical Society

TABLE OF CONTENTS

Preface

What a find! Last summer, while antique shopping and book browsing in Benton, PA, I spotted a church cookbook titled: *RECIPES: Collected by the Ladies of the Presbyterian Church of Kingston, Pennsylvania* Although cooking is not my thing, Kingston, PA is my home town and I am always interested in local history. So I picked up the little hardcover book and thought: "Hey, this is pretty neat." Examining the book a bit closer, I saw that it was published in "1907." My thoughts immediately went from "Hey" to "Wow"! I had found a one-hundred and five year-old historical treasure of Kingston.

Looking through the book, I recognized the last names of many of the ladies who submitted their recipes; names like "Loveland," "Hoyt," "Dorrance," and "Vaughn." These names are familiar to me because they are the names of Kingston streets. For example, when I was in grade school and high school my family lived at the corner of Wyoming Avenue and East Vaughn Street. Reading the recipes submitted by Mrs. Vaughn took me back to my Mom's home cooking.

Following is a list of ladies whose last name is also the name of a current Kingston street:

Mrs. R. B. Vaughn
Mrs. H. H. Welles, Jr.
Miss Augusta Hoyt
S. S. Goodwin
Mrs. Abram Goodwin
Miss Elizabeth Loveland
Miss Frances Dorrance
Mrs. T. W. Thomas
Mrs. Newitt
Mrs. W. F. Church
Mrs. Brewster

Mrs. Pierce Butler
Mrs. J. Ford Dorrance.

I was also interested to find names of ladies who may have
been the grandmothers or great grandmothers of
individuals I knew when I attended Kingston High School
in the 1960s.
For example:

Mrs. Hilbert (Donald – teacher and track coach)
Mrs. M. A. Scureman (Mark - student)
Mrs. Benner (Johnny - student)
Mrs. E. R. Morgan (Bill - teacher, Phil - teacher and Barry -
student)
Mrs. D. H. Lake (Donny - student)
Mrs. John E. Jenkins (Maude - student)
Mrs. W.L. Dean (Ron - student).

As someone unfamiliar with cooking, some of the recipe
ingredients and/or instructions made me wonder and
often chuckle:

"saltpeter size of a walnut"
"put butter in spider"
"1 gill of wine"
"bake in a … ramekin"
"beaf loaf"
"a shin of beef"
"bake until done"
"N.O. molasses"
"roll the dough for one hour"
"gem tins"
"butter size of an egg"
"butter size of a walnut"
"Pork cake."

And my personal favorite: "butter size of a turkey egg."

The covers of my copy of *RECIPES* are a bit edge worn and

the pages are slightly browned. However, for a 105 year old book it is in quite good condition. The book is case-bound with cloth hard covers and has 183 numbered pages, plus many blank pages for notes. In total, it contains over 450 recipes collected by 96 ladies of the Kingston Presbyterian Church.

After leafing through the book, I decided to scan the text of *RECIPES* and create a new book in digital format. It took me approximately 20 hours to scan and edit what I had scanned. While my copy of *RECIPES* is generally in good condition, some of the pages are a bit faded so the scanning process was somewhat tedious. It was also my first foray into "scanning," and I did pile up more than a few learning-curve hours.

The more time I spent scanning *RECIPES* the more interested I became in the ladies who contributed to the book. What was life like in the United States and Kingston, Pennsylvania in 1907? Who were the ladies of the Presbyterian Church of Kingston? What were their first names? How old were they? What were their homes like? Who were their spouses and did they have children? What were their interests? Which one of the ladies led the publication of *RECIPES*?

I try to answer these questions in the following pages. I hope you enjoy both the recipes and the bit of historical context that I was able to find. Please send your corrections and comments to me at rws23@ptd.net.

Robert W. Surridge, D.Ed.
Kingston, Pennsylvania
August 2012

Dedication - To My Hero

My maternal grandmother was Mrs. Charles R. (Beatrice)
Struble. Born in 1884, she was the daughter of English
immigrants and a lifelong resident of Scranton, PA.
Grandma Struble lived to be 99 years old and survived my
grandfather by 57 years. Yet, until her death in 1983 she
remained Mrs. Charles R. Struble. As a widow, she raised
my mother, Lois, and my aunt Esther through the perilous
days of the Great Depression. I have wonderful memories
and great respect for my caring and strong-willed
grandmother who has always been my greatest hero!

Mr. and Mrs. Charles R. Struble and Lois Struble - 1913

Introduction

In the words of Ruth Reichl, Culinary Editor, *Modern Library,* to fully appreciate a vintage cookbook, the challenge is not just to cook the recipes, but to "read through the recipes to the lives behind them."[1] The following is intended to help readers meet this challenge.

However, before reading into the lives of the ladies of Kingston Presbyterian Church, the reader may appreciate having some background information about Kingston, Pennsylvania. The Borough of Kingston is located in Luzerne County in northeastern Pennsylvania, approximately 100 miles north of Philadelphia. It is one of the older European communities in the state established before the Revolutionary War by migrants from Connecticut. Until the late 1700s, Kingston and the surrounding area was claimed by Connecticut, as well as Pennsylvania.

Kingston was incorporated in 1857 with a total population of 598 residents. It was incorporated, in large part, due to the then recent construction and opening of the Lackawanna and Bloomsburg Railroad, as well as the continuing development of the Wyoming Seminary School. The school was established in 1844, and by 1857 had the beginnings of its exceptional reputation for preparing students for success at the most prestigious and selective colleges and universities in the United States.

The year 1907 was Kingston's fiftieth anniversary and it was then home to approximately 6,000 residents.[2] In 1921, Kingston consolidated with neighboring Dorranceton Borough and the approximate boundaries of modern Kingston were established. By the time of its centennial celebration in 1957, the population of the Borough of Kingston was near 21,000 residents.[3]

To address Reichl's challenge of "reading through the recipes," the following narrative is divided into five parts. The first part provides the reader with background information about the United States during the Progressive Era (1890-1920). The second part describes local events during the early 1900s in Luzerne County and Kingston. The third part provides details about the lives of the women who contributed to *RECIPES*. The fourth part contains information and advice helpful to cooking these vintage recipes. The final part contains the complete text of *RECIPES* and includes over 450 recipes.

Map of Kingston

The author was unable to find a map of the Borough of Kingston from the early 1900s. Subsequently, the author developed the following map to depict the approximate boundaries of the Borough of Kingston in 1910. The map is based on a combination of information drawn from an unnamed 1883 map provided by the Luzerne County Historical Society and the listing of Kingston streets found in the household records of the 1910 Federal Census.

Part One: America in 1907

The Progressive Era

In 1907, Theodore "Teddy" Roosevelt, the 26th president of the United States (1901–1909), was fully engaged in the political and social reforms of the Progressive Era. With his bigger than life "roughrider" persona, Roosevelt was a Republican who coined the phrase "square deal" to describe his efforts to build middle-class America.

Roosevelt led national efforts to rein-in the growing power of large trusts (corporations). In 1902, the "trustbuster" intervened to help settle Pennsylvania's Great Anthracite Strike of coal miners. Roosevelt urged mine owners to negotiate with the United Mine Workers Union. The strike ended with the workers receiving more pay for fewer hours of work.

Along with political and social reform, Progressive Era activists promoted the achievement of efficiency in all sectors of the economy. They believed that modernization and improvement would result from the application of scientific solutions to all types of human endeavors.

Business and industry embraced "scientific management" to improve worker efficiency. Higher education continued to develop the "social sciences," and university professors took on more responsibility to become "research faculty" with an expanded mission of teaching, plus research and service. Rural residents turned to new methods of "modern agriculture," and the "City Beautiful" movement sought ways to make urban living healthier for industrial workers.

Before the end of the Progressive Era there would be four new amendments to the U. S. Constitution:

1913 – 16th Amendment – National income tax
1913 – 17th Amendment – Direct election of senators
1919 – 18th Amendment – Prohibition
1920 – 19th Amendment – Women's Suffrage.

New Immigrants

In the first decade of the 1900s, nearly 9 million "new immigrants" entered the United States. They were seen to be much different from the earlier immigrants who were mostly Protestants from northern and western Europe. Many of the new immigrants were Catholic or Jewish and came from countries in eastern and southern Europe, as well as Ireland.

During this period, more men were always needed to work in factories, foundries and the coal mines. Most of these men came from the ranks of new immigrants. Before 1924, immigration into the United States for Europeans was a comparatively straight forward affair. The eight-to-fourteen day trip across the Atlantic was certainly arduous. However, once a European immigrant was deemed by immigration officials to be healthy and not a criminal, she or he was generally admitted into the country. Indeed, during the peak period of immigration only 2% to 3% of immigrants annually were denied entrance to America.[4] While the new immigrants were often unskilled and many could only speak a few words of English, they were liberally admitted into the United States. Nationally, there were so many new immigrants that the country's established population of Anglo-Americans or "old immigrants," complained that the United States was a "dumping ground" for Europe's uneducated and unskilled.

The years 1906 and 1907 were the peak years of immigration. On January 5, 1907, the Wilkes-Barre Record newspaper reported that the country's Commissioner General of Immigration had stated that: "The physical and mental quality of people we are now receiving is much below that of those who have come in former years." In 1911, the United States Immigration Commission stated that immigrants from southern and eastern Europe were a serious threat to American society and culture. The Commission concluded that the number of these immigrants coming into the country should be greatly reduced. The Emergency Quota Act in 1921 and the Immigration Act of 1924, were both aimed at restricting the number of southern and eastern European immigrants. In 1924, quotas were set for European immigrants so that no more than 3% of the number of pre-1890 immigrants from any country was allowed into the United States. The new quota annually allowed about 4,000 immigrants from Italy and approximately 6,000 from Poland. In comparison, the annual quotas for Great Britain and Germany were 34,000 and 50,000 per year, respectively.[5] Obviously, the new immigration laws greatly reduced the number of southern and eastern Europeans entering the county.

American Happenings[6]

The following notes are provided to give the reader a general idea of the nature of American life in the early twentieth century.

- Only 14% of the homes had a bathtub and only 8 percent of the homes had a telephone.
- The average wage in 1907 was 22 cents per hour and the average laborer made between $200 and $400 per year.
- A competent accountant could expect to earn $2000 per year, a dentist $2,500 per year, a veterinarian between $1,500 and $4,000 per year, and a mechanical engineer about $5,000 per year.
- Sugar cost four cents a pound, eggs were fourteen cents a dozen, and coffee was fifteen cents a pound.
- Most women only washed their hair once a month, and used Borax or egg yolks for shampoo.

- The average life expectancy was 46 years for men and 50 years for women.
- Five leading causes of death were:
    1. Pneumonia and influenza
    2. Tuberculosis
    3. Diarrhea
    4. Heart disease
    5. Stroke.
- Only 6% of all Americans had graduated from high school.
- Marijuana, heroin, and morphine were all available over the counter at the local corner drugstores. Pharmacists said, 'Heroin clears the complexion, gives buoyancy to the mind, regulates the stomach and bowels, and is, in fact, a perfect guardian of health."
- Eighteen percent of households had at least one full-time servant or domestic help.
- There were about 230 reported murders in the entire United States.
- Congress raised their annual salaries to $7,500.
- Panic of 1907: A run on Knickerbocker Trust Company stock sets events in motion that led to a depression.
- Chicago Cubs defeated Detroit (4-0-1) in the World Series; Yale was the college football champion; Pink Star won the Kentucky Derby.
- New songs of 1907 included: Auld Lang Syne, My Gal Sal, Harrigan, My Wild Irish Rose, and School Days.

Part Two: Luzerne County and Kingston in 1907

Local Events

Several significant events occurred in Kingston and Luzerne County between 1901 and 1907. The most notable was the Great Anthracite Coal Strike of 1902. According to the Wilkes-Barre Record newspaper it was the largest strike in world history. Also of significance, the Susquehanna River flooded many Kingston residents each year from 1901 to 1904. The flood of 1904 was reported as the most serious flood in local memory. Community health was always a concern in the early 1900s. Kingston residents were certainly cognizant of the danger of disease outbreaks such as the 1905 typhoid fever epidemic, in the nearby town of Nanticoke. This epidemic accounted for a total of 512 cases leading to 46 deaths.

Following are some of the events reported in the 1908 Wilkes-Barre Record Almanac for Luzerne County in 1907:

- "Luzerne County during 1907 shared with the rest of the country in the wave of prosperity (p. 20)."
- "There were quite a few serious mine accidents during the year. In February seven men were suffocated by fire in No. 19 mine of the Lehigh & Wilkes-Barre Coal Co. and in July, nine men were suffocated by white damp in the Audenried mine of the same company. Four men were killed by a cave-in in No. 14 mine of the Pennsylvania Coal Co. at Port Blanchard in August, and in September four men were killed in the South Wilkes-Barre Mine of the Lehigh & Wilkes-Barre (p.20)."
- "Ten men and boys were drowned while bathing during the summer, the same numbers as the year previous (p. 20)."
- "January 24 the thermometer registered 3 below zero in Wilkes-Barre and 18 below at Bear Creek. On that date the river closed for the second time during the winter, and it remained closed until near the middle

of March. There was a frost during every month of the year, a most unusual occurrence (p. 20)."

- "In February twenty-five alleged members of the Black Hand in the Pittston region were arrested by the county detectives, the Pittston police and members of the State constabulary, charged with having been responsible for dynamiting, shooting, attempting to extort money, etc. (p. 21)."
- "More equitable valuation of property for purposes of taxation caused a great deal of interest in Luzerne County during 1907, and the Record took a prominent part in the agitation (p. 22)."
- "The agitation was begun by the very apparent negligence on the part of assessors. It was well known that coal land was not assessed in proportion to the value placed upon other property, and that the real estate assessments varied greatly-the whole resulting in a very unfair distribution of the burdens of taxation. It was generally known the small property owner that was discriminated against in favor of the large property owner (p. 22)."

Events of 1907 specific to Kingston recorded in the 1908 Wilkes-Barre Record Almanac include the following:

- "Luzerne county Women's Christian Temperance Union (W.C.T, U.) Convention in Kingston (p. 106)."
- "The Kingston Coal Co., was restrained by court order from robbing pillars under St. Vincent's cemetery in Plymouth (P. 109)."
- "Thomas Coolbaugh, a Kingston young man, dies from bullet wound (p. 110)."
- "Fred E. Zerbey, connected with the Lehigh Valley Coal Co., takes the position of general manager for the Kingston Coal Co., made vacant by the death of Robert S. Mercur (p. 112)."
- "Rutter's grove donated to the Wilkes-Barre Park Commission by President Underwood of the Erie Railroad and Abram Nesbitt of Kingston."
- "Dr. E. H. Coolbaugh of Kingston found dead in the woods at Harvey's Lake, where he had gone to hunt,

death having been caused probably by heart disease (p. 115)."
- "Opening recital on the new pipe organ in St. Ignatius Catholic Church, Kingston (p. 117)."
- "In June T. L. Newell, of Kingston, donated a farm near Harvey's Lake for the use of boys during the summer, and several camping parties pitched tents under the supervision of Rev. Mr. Sweet, who had charge of the place (p. 113)."

Accidental Death

Numerous accidental deaths reflected the realities of life in the early 1900s. The reports of accidental deaths in the 1908 Wilkes-Barre Record Almanac suggest that the surest path to accidental death was employment in a coal mine. In 1907, there were 194 coal mine deaths in Luzerne County. Two Kingston men were among this number. Thomas Lusky and Frank Winters were killed in coal mine accidents (pages 55-56).

Also reported by the Wilkes-Barre Record Almanac was accidental death from a range of causes such as fire, poisoning, industrial accidents, drowning, dog bites, and household accidents. One hundred and seventeen (117) of these types of fatal accidents were recorded. Only one person living in Kingston was among this number. Thomas J. Lewis, 41 years, died after his clothing caught in machinery in the Kingston Manufacturing Company's plant (p. 57).

Sixty-two railroad deaths occurred in 1907. Kingston's William Gredas and Joseph Urban died from accidents at the D. L. & W. and the Lehigh Valley railroads, respectively (p. 55). There were also 13 people murdered in Luzerne County during 1907. None of the victims was a resident of Kingston (p. 55).

Kingston's New Immigrants

By 1914, there were 181,000 miners employed in the

Anthracite mines of Northeast Pennsylvania.[7] The promise of jobs in the coal mines brought many new immigrants to Kingston and the rest of Luzerne County. Between 1890 and 1910, Luzerne County's population increased by 71% from 201,203 persons to 343,186 persons.[8] During the same period, Kingston's percentage increase was an even more dramatic 179%. Kingston's population grew from 2,381 residents in 1890 to 6,649 in 1910.[9]

By 1910, 64% of Kingston's population was either foreign born (30%) or had at least one parent who was foreign born (34%).[10] For small communities like Kingston, the published reports from the 1910 U. S. Census do not detail the number of immigrants coming from each foreign country. Fortunately, the 1910 Census reports do provide this information at the county level. In 1910 a total of 98,607 foreign born individuals lived in Luzerne County. Of this number, 72,646 or 74% immigrated to the United States from Ireland (6,752) or the eastern and southern European countries of Russia (28,015), Austria (23,375)[11], Italy (9,368), and Hungary (5,136). Most of the other foreign born residents migrated to Luzerne County from Germany (8,871); Wales (7,324), England (6,431) and Scotland (1,283).[12]

The Wilkes-Barre Record newspaper often used the term "foreigners" when referring to the new immigrants. Following are examples of how the lives of the "foreigners," were described during 1906 and 1907 by the local newspaper:

- "Seven Mocanaqua foreigners arrested by the State constabulary for interfering with workingmen at the West End Coal Co. (April 26, 1906.)"
- "Drunken fight among foreigners near Pittston results in the injury of some of the foreigners and two of the State Constabulary force (August 19, 1906)."

- "Foreigners at Luzerne Borough engage in drunken riot in a saloon and the State constabulary called upon (August 27, 1906)."
- "Two foreigners charged with dynamiting Lehigh Valley train in April arrested (November 3, 1906)."
- "A foreigner shot to death near Sugar Notch in a fight between game warden and his friends and a party of foreigners (September 8, 1906)."
- "Two murders – one at Pittston and the other at Inkerman, both of the victims being foreigners (December 17, 1906)."
- "Frank Pypsey, a foreigner of Dupont, died at the Pittston hospital from fracture of the skull, sustained a few days previously by a stone thrown by some unknown party while he was on his way home. He had been drinking in a saloon (December 21, 1906)."
- "Michael Keriz of Pittston was beaten to death with a baseball bat near his home, during a quarrel. Four foreigners were arrested (July 14, 1907)."
- "Leo Boner, a young Italian of Wilkes-Barre, was shot through the heart during a wedding celebration, which ended in a fight. His brother, John Boner, was arrested. The shooting was done with a gun. It was alleged that the shot was intended for some one else (September 18, 1907)."[13]

Kingston Businesses

Appendix A lists Kingston businesses identified in the 1902 Purdon's Wilkes-Barre/Scranton Business Directory. The business district in Kingston was rather small with stores located in a four-to-five block area around West Market Street, Main Street and Wyoming Avenue.

Looking through the table it is interesting to note the number of businesses selling similar products. For example:
- Saloon – 6 listings, plus 4 other listings selling wine or liquor
- Bakery/Confectionary - 9 listings
- Barber – 7 listings

- Grocery/Market – 7 listings
- Hotels – 3 listings

Kingstonian's of 1907 did not limit their shopping to Kingston. Shoppers could also go to the City of Wilkes-Barre, which is located across the Susquehanna River from Kingston. In 1907, Wilkes-Barre was booming and in 1910 it was ranked among the 100 largest communities in the country[14]. Kingston and Wilkes-Barre were linked by an excellent electric street car system, which allowed workers and shoppers to easily travel to and from Kingston and Wilkes-Barre. Awaiting them were a number of stores such as the Boston Store (now Boscov's Department Store), Issac Long's, Kirby's Five and Ten, Simon Long's & Son, Lazarus Bros., The Globe, Weitzenkorns, and the Bee Hive. These stores and myriad others were thriving in the city's downtown shopping district. Men's suits were available for as little as $6.50, women's suits for $7.98, mink scarves sold for $4.98, men's overcoats for $10 to $15. Many of the stores also provided customers with Green Stamps with purchases. Undoubtedly, some individuals also found the goods they needed by shopping in catalogs. It is estimated that the Sears Roebuck and Montgomery Ward catalogs were read more than any other book except the Bible.

Wilkes-Barre also provided opportunities for entertainment. Live theater and performances were available at the Nesbitt Theater and the Grand Opera House. These venues attracted headliners like Lillian Russell and John Phillip Sousa. Each theater boasted a full schedule of performances. The following table lists the performances in each theater for just the month of January 1907.

Wilkes-Barre Theaters Attractions – January 1907

The Nesbitt	Grand Opera House
The Girl from Broadway	A Desperate Chance
The Gingerbread Man	The Flaming Arrow
Simple, Simon, Simple	The Eye Witness
The Education of Mr. Pipp	Human Hearts
O'Brien-Burns Fight (moving pictures)	A Race for Life
The Spring Chicken	A Wife's Secret
The Embassy Ball	The Cowboy Girl
His Honor the Mayor	A Man's Broken Promise
The Volunteer Organist	Happy Hooligan
The Medicine Man	For a Human Life
Al Fields's Minstrels	
Too Near Home	
Chester D'Amon and Vaudeville	

The Hotel Sterling, which was constructed in 1898 with 175 rooms and 125 bathrooms, was the leading hotel in the area. The hotel's meeting and banquet rooms provided a venue for a variety of social and business events.

Meetings, receptions, weddings, and banquets were also held at prestigious private clubs such as the Franklin Club and the Westmoreland Club, both located on South Franklin Street in Wilkes-Barre.

Kingston Homes
Following are photographs of houses where some of the ladies resided in 1907. While many of the ladies' houses remain family homes, a good number currently house businesses covering a range of enterprises from offices for

attorneys and physicians, to beauty shops and retail stores.

The typical house is a two-to-three story Victorian era structure. Many have large porches, turrets and bay windows. In 1907, most of these houses had a coal furnace to produce heat and hot water. Some of these systems also included a small "bucket-a-day" furnace for heating hot water in the summer months. Although by 1907 gas cook stoves were becoming available, cooking was most often done on a cast-iron coal cook stove. Having a toasty warm kitchen was an added winter benefit of the coal stove, but a bit of detraction in warmer weather. Food was kept fresh in an icebox refrigerator which, of course, required the regular delivery of ice to the home.

In 1907, the ladies' homes most likely had one or two bathrooms and a telephone. Most, if not all, of the homes had electric lights with power provided by the West Side Electric Light Company established in 1893.[15]

2012 Photographs of Selected Former Residences

Former Residence of Miss Elizabeth Loveland – 2012

Former Residence of Mrs. Sofia Cooper- 2012

Former Residence of Mrs. Josephine Darte - 2012

Former Residence of Miss Esther French – 2012

Former Residence of Mrs. Sophia S. Goodwin – 2012

Former Residence of Mrs. Mary Rosser – 2012

Former Residence of Mary A. Van Scoy -2012

Presbyterian Church of Kingston

The history of the church dates back to 1819, when local ministers organized a Congregationalist church with 24 members. The church officially became Presbyterian in 1823. The first church edifice was constructed on Wyoming Avenue in 1842. In 1875, the second edifice was built at the corner of North Maple Avenue and North Market Streets in Kingston. Use of this church building, was discontinued after the Agnes Flood in 1972.[16]

Following the flood, the Presbyterian congregation joined with a local Methodist congregation to create the Church of Christ Uniting, which is located at the corner of North Market Street and Sprague Avenue in Kingston. Over its 153 year history, five other churches were formed from the Presbyterian Church of Kingston. The last was the Magyar (Hungarian) Presbyterian Church of Westmoor, which was established in 1901.[17]

In 1907, Rev. Ferdinand von Krug was nearing the end of his tenure as the longtime pastor of the Kingston Presbyterian church. He served as pastor for twenty-two years from 1886 to 1908. Following is an 1893 biographical sketch of Reverend von Krug from <u>The History of Luzerne County Pennsylvania,</u> H. C. Bradsby, Editor. S. B. Nelson & Co., Publishers, 1893.

REV. FERDINAND VON KRUG, Presbyterian minister, Kingston, was born in Germany, January 26, 1850, and is a son of Jacob and Mary (Otto) Von Krug. He was educated in the schools of Darmstadt and Heidelberg, in his native land, and in 1869 came to America, where he attended the Western Reserve College, graduating therefrom in 1873, in which year he proceeded to Auburn, N.Y., where he remained three years, receiving his theological education. He then went to Bloomingburg, Ohio, and was there engaged in ministerial work from 1876 to 1884, and then moving to White Haven, Pa., he remained there about two years, when he came to Kingston, where he has since been located. Mr. Von Krug was married, in 1876, to Miss Welitta Barnes, of Rock Stream, N.Y. and they have three children: Harry, Karl and Mary. He is a member of the F.& A.M.

Part Three: The Ladies of the Presbyterian Church

The Ladies

Ninety-six ladies collected recipes and contributed to the
RECIPES cookbook. Appendix B contains detailed
information about 75 of the 96 ladies. It was built using
household records from the 1910 U. S. Federal Census.

Reviewing the information in Appendix B allows readers
to become familiar with several details about the lives of
the ladies. As noted above, the author was able to identify
the household records for 75 of the 96 ladies. There are
several reasons why information about the other 21 ladies
was not found in the Census records. The 1910 Census
was taken three years after *RECIPES* was published
making it a possibility that some of the ladies had moved
to other communities, some may have passed away,
unmarried ladies may have married in the interim, some
households may not have participated in the Census, or
some of the ladies may have divorced. The author's
limited skill as a data detective is certainly another reason
why some of the ladies remain mostly anonymous.

The 1910 Federal Census records provide a great deal of
information about each person in an enumerated
household. The information includes:
1. State, county and town of residence;
2. Street address;
3. Name and relationship to the Head-of-Household;
4. Sex and Age at last birthday;
5. Marital status;
6. Place of birth;
7. Father's place of birth;
8. Mother's place of birth; and
9. Occupation.

Most of the ladies resided in either the Borough of
Kingston or the neighboring communities of Dorranceton

and Forty Fort. A few of the ladies lived in Wilkes-Barre, Wyoming and West Pittston. None of the ladies lived in the adjacent town of Edwardsville. The person identified as the Head-of-Household was usually a husband, father, brother or son. Five of the ladies, namely Miss Elizabeth Loveland, Mrs. Mary A. Van Scoy, Miss Anna Raub, Miss Katharine Parsons, and Mrs. Laura Diggory were listed as Head-of-Household.

In 1907, the average age of the ladies was 42 years. At 70 years of age, Mrs. Franck was the oldest contributor. Mrs. Edith Snow at 17 was the youngest. Miss Elizabeth Loveland contributed the most recipes (25) followed closely by Miss Jesse Macfarlane who contributed 22.

Eighty-four percent of the ladies were married or widowed. Nearly all of these ladies used their husband's initials or first name to identify themselves in *RECIPES*. For example, Bertha Buckman was identified as Mrs. E. E. Buckman and Mary Butler was listed as Mrs. Pierce Butler. Two ladies may have been making a statement of future liberation by using their own first initials instead of their husband's initials. Mrs. S. S. Goodwin was Mrs. Sophia S. Goodwin and Julia D. Flanagan identified herself as Mrs. J. D. Flanagan. Most unmarried ladies used their full first and last name to identify themselves; for instance, Miss Elizabeth Loveland, Miss Jesse MacFarlane, and Miss Augusta Hoyt.

Thirty-two of the 75 households (43%) contained individuals whose occupation was listed as a servant on the 1910 Census form. At least one of the ladies who contributed to *RECIPES* was a household servant employed by another contributor. Mrs. Bessie Benner is identified in the 1910 Census as a servant in the Van Scoy household.

There were a total of 118 children living in the 75 households. Eighty-one children were 18 years old or younger. Mr. and Mrs. R. P. Brodhead had six children under 17-years old at home in 1907. According to the Census records, only three of the ladies worked outside of the home. Miss Helen Goodwin and Miss Katharine Parsons were school teachers and Miss Nellie Grover worked as a seamstress. From other sources it was determined that Miss Frances Dorrance was employed as a librarian.

All but six of the ladies were born in the United States. The ladies who were not native born were born in Germany, England, Wales, Scotland and two ladies were born in Canada. All the ladies' surnames are of western or northern European origin. With few exceptions, their husbands, fathers, brothers and sons worked in professional positions such as lawyers, physicians, bankers, engineers, real estate agents, merchants, land holding farmers, railroad agents, or coal mining executives. Only one spouse was employed as a coal miner.

Personal and Family Notes

The following provides additional detail about the lives of the ladies. Readers will note that much of the detail is not about the ladies, but about their parents, siblings, husbands, sons and daughters. The major reason for this shortcoming is the scarcity of information available about the ladies themselves. However, it seems appropriate to use this surrogate information to depict the lives of the ladies as the activities and accomplishments of our loved ones are often a reflection of our own lives and aspirations.

Education

- Mrs. C. W. (Anne) Bixby's husband Charles graduated from Lafayette University. In 1907, her son Edward graduated from Princeton University. In 1911 he graduated from the Pennsylvania Medical School and later became a staff physician at Wilkes-

Barre's General Hospital rising to the position of Chief, Medical Services.

- Mrs. E. E. (Bertha) Buckman's father Dr. Edward Bannister in 1860 was named the president of the University of the Pacific. Originally from the state of New York, Dr. Bannister sent three of his daughters Clara, Alice, and Bertha to study at Syracuse University. After graduating from Syracuse, each of the sisters came to Kingston to teach at Wyoming Seminary. Clara from 1876 to 1881, Alice from 1881 to 1894, and Bertha from 1887 to 1894. Both Bertha and her sister Alice met their future husbands while at Seminary. Alice met John H. Race who graduated from Wyoming Seminary in 1886. After graduation from Princeton in 1890, Race was ordained as a Methodist Episcopal minister and taught Greek rhetoric at Wyoming Seminary from 1890 to 1894. Later he became the president of the University of Chattanooga. Bertha also met her husband Elmer E. Buckman while she was teaching at Wyoming Seminary. Mr. Buckman later became the vice-president of a local bank.
- Mrs. Pierce (Mary) Butler's foster daughter Charlotte Beardier was a public school teacher.
- Mrs. W. F. (Anna) Church's daughter Elizabeth was a 1905 graduate of Cornell University. In 1911, Elizabeth took a position teaching mathematics at Wyoming Seminary. Mrs. Church's youngest child, Frederick Corss Church also graduated from Cornell University. After his Cornell graduation, he taught at Penn State College until World War I. During the war, he served as the director of the YMCA in Italy. In 1921, he accepted Idaho University's offer of $2,100 to join their history department. He retired from his faculty position at Idaho in 1955.
- Mrs. Frederick (Martha) Corss's husband graduated from Lafayette College in 1861. He also served as a faculty member at Wyoming Seminary.
- Mrs. W. L. (Mary G.) Dean's husband Willis L. Dean came to Wyoming Seminary in 1875 as Professor of Penmanship. In a short time he became the director of the business school and retired in 1942 completing

sixty-seven (67) years of service at Wyoming Seminary. In 1943, his daughter Mrs. George W. Carey established the Wyoming Seminary Willis L. Dean Citizenship Prizes in memory of her father.

- Mrs. J. Ford (Elizabeth) Dorrance's husband John graduated from Lehigh University in 1871.
- Miss Frances Dorrance graduated from Wyoming Seminary in 1896 and Vassar College in 1890. She also studied German for three semesters at Berlin University. She received a degree in library science from the New York State Library School.
- Mrs. D. H. (Elisa) Eavenson's youngest daughter Anna became a supervising registered nurse at Geisinger Hospital in Danville, PA.
- Miss Helen Goodwin and Miss Katharine Parsons were school teachers.
- Mrs. George (Alice) Ives' oldest daughter Marion attended the St. Stevens Boarding School for Girls in Catonsville, Maryland.
- Mrs. (Anna) Grover's son Alfred graduated from Wyoming Seminary and Albany (New York) Medical School.
- Mrs. John E. (Katharine) Jenkins's son Mitchell graduated from Wesleyan University in 1919 and New York University School of Law in 1923.
- Mrs. S. E. (Grace) Leacock was a school teacher.
- Mrs. John (Fidelia) Nugent's son Harold graduated from Cornell University in 1907.
- Mrs. M. D. (Mary) Rosser's husband David graduated from Cornell University in 1895.
- Mrs. Mark A. (Blanche) Scureman's daughter Dorothy was a school teacher.
- Mrs. B. R. (Carrie) Tubbs's daughter Clara was a school teacher.
- Mrs. R. B. (Rilla) Vaughn's daughter Florence was a school teacher.

Public Service
- Mrs. C. (Sarah) Bach's husband Christian served as the Postmaster at the Kingston Post Office.

- Mrs. (Sofia) Cooper, Mrs. J. D. (Julia) Flanagan, and Mrs. John (Fidelia) Nugent's husbands served as members of Kingston Borough Council.
- Mrs. J. Ford (Elizabeth) Dorrance's husband John served as a member of Pennsylvania Governor Henry Martyn Hoyt's staff.
- Mrs. (Elizabeth) Frane's husband William was a clerk at the Kingston Post Office.
- Mrs. (Elizabeth) Gregory's husband William served as the Chief-of-Police for Kingston Borough.
- Mrs. (Anna) Grover's son Alfred was a member of the Kingston School Board for twenty years and the president of the Board for ten years.
- Miss Augusta Hoyt, Mrs. George (Anna) Hoyt Shoemaker and Mrs. Frederick (Martha) Hoyt Corss were nieces of Henry Martyn Hoyt, Sr. Mr. Hoyt was the 18th Governor of Pennsylvania from 1879 to 1883, as well as a general in the Union army during the American Civil War.
- Mrs. John E. (Katharine) Jenkins's oldest son Mitchell served in the U.S. Congress from 1947 to 1949. He was preceded and succeeded in Congress by Daniel J. Flood. Mr. Jenkins also served several years as the assistant district attorney of Luzerne County.
- Mrs. George (Amanda) Lewis's husband was a laborer employed by Kingston Borough.
- Mrs. George (Anna) Shoemaker's husband was a member of Forty Fort Borough Council.
- Mrs. R. B. (Rilla) Vaughn's husband served as the Fire Chief in Kingston Borough.

Military Service
- Miss Nellie Parry's father was a veteran of the Civil War.
- Mrs. L. C. (Josephine) Darte's husband, brother-in-law, and father-in-law were veterans of the Civil War.
- Miss Esther French's brother Charles was a veteran of the Spanish/American War.

- Mrs. E. G. (Margaret) Gage's husband Erastus was a captain in the Pennsylvania National Guard and was activated to serve in the Spanish/American War.
- Mrs. C. W. (Anne) Bixby's son Edward was a member of the Pennsylvania National Guard and was on active duty on the Mexican border in 1916 and 1917. He later served in France with the 109th Field Artillery rising to the rank of Captain. The army awarded him the highest rating of any surgeon in the National Guard.
- Mrs. (Janette) Newitt's son George was killed in action at Chateau Thierry in World War I. Mr. and Mrs. Newitt later presented a bronze tablet at the Kingston Presbyterian Church in memory of their son.
- Mrs. M. D. (Mary) Rosser's son Charles was a veteran of World War I.
- Mrs. R. P. (Fannie) Brodhead's son Francis was a veteran of World War I. He arrived overseas in 1918. He was promoted from private to corporal, December 10, 1918, and from corporal to sergeant in February 24, 1919.
- Mrs. Mark A. (Blanche) Scureman's son Harry was a veteran of World War I.
- Mrs. J. G. (Margaret) Sperlings' son Frederick was a veteran of World War I.
- Mrs. John E. (Katharine) Jenkins's son Mitchell in 1917 enlisted as a private in the United States Army and was discharged as a first lieutenant on January 2, 1919. He enlisted in the Pennsylvania National Guard as a private in January 1926 and rose through the ranks to lieutenant colonel prior to induction into Federal service on February 17, 1941. He served four and a one-half years in World War II during which time he was promoted to colonel, and was placed on inactive status on October 5, 1945. He retired as a brigadier general in the Pennsylvania National Guard.
- Mrs. George F. (Phebe) Lee's daughter Phebe Jr. was a Captain in the Women's Army Auxiliary Corp during World War II.

Community Notables

- Mrs. R. P. (Fannie) Brodhead, Miss Elizabeth Loveland, Mrs. M. E. (Bertha) Marvin, and Mrs. Andrew Raub were among a group of twelve women who in 1903 organized a women's civic organization that was the beginning of today's Wyoming Valley Women's Club.

- Miss Frances Dorrance served as the director of Wyoming Historical and Geological Society (now the Luzerne County Historical Society). She also was a librarian at Wilkes College, director of the Back Mountain (Pennsylvania) Library, and director of the Hoyt Library in Kingston from 1928 to her retirement. She was the first woman in the nation to receive the Distinguished Service Citation from the American Legion. She was designated as a Distinguished Daughter of the Commonwealth of Pennsylvania in 1952. In 1970, she was the recipient of the J. Alden Mason award from the Pennsylvania Society of Archeology. She also received the Distinguished Service Award from Wyoming Seminary.

- Mr. and Mrs. R. P. (Fannie) Brodhead and Miss Elizabeth Loveland in 1917 presented the Kingston Presbyterian Church with a new organ in memory of their mother Mrs. Mary Buckingham Loveland.

- Mrs. Wesley (Hattie) Hilbert in 1919 was the president of the Presbyterian Woman's Home Mission Society.

- Miss Elizabeth Loveland served as a vice-president of the Presbyterian Women's Foreign Mission Society.

- Mrs. R. P. (Fannie) Brodhead's husband Robert was the chairman of the organizing committee of the Rotary Club of Wilkes-Barre in 1915. Robert was also a member of the Holland Society of New York.

- Mrs. E. E. (Bertha) Buckman's husband Elmer was the cashier and vice president of the Wyoming National Bank.

- Mrs. (Mary) Brewster's husband William was the solicitor of Kingston High School from 1909 to 1948. He also authored The Certified Township of

<u>Kingston Pennsylvania, 1769 to 1929</u>, which was published by the School District of Kingston in 1930.

- Mrs. (Anna) Grover's son Alfred practiced medicine for over 50 years and was a member of the staff at Nesbitt Memorial Hospital in Kingston.
- Miss (Elizabeth and Anna) Lawley's brother Richard was a music publisher and he wrote the words and music to the song "We see Red, White and Blue" in 1944.
- Mrs. (Lucy) Murdock's husband Leonard was the pastor of the Kingston Methodist Episcopal Church from 1897 to 1905
- Mrs. F. L. (Mary) Olds' husband Frederick was an architect who designed Wilkes-Barre's Wheelman's Club, later known as the Franklin Club, on South Franklin Street in Wilkes-Barre, PA. The building is on the National Register of Historic Buildings. In the 1880s, Mr. Olds designed several buildings at the Pennsylvania State University.
- Mrs. F. L. (Mary) Olds's children Carolyn Olds (17), Kate Talbot Olds (15), and Sarah Olds (11) attended school in Brussels, Belgium. Because of the 1914 invasion of Belgium by the German army they were part of a group of fifteen girls forced to quickly leave Belgium for England. After landing in England, they were left stranded hungry and penniless on the London docks. After several hours, a society of American women in London took charge of the children until family arrangements could be realized.
- Mrs. R. P. (Fannie) Brodhead and her husband Robert were married in 1889. Following is a copy of

their marriage announcement.

A KINGSTON WEDDING.

ROBERT P. BRODHEAD MARRIES MISS FANNY VAUGHN
LOVELAND.

The residence of William Loveland, of Kingston, was the
scene of a pretty wedding yesterday, the occasion being the marriage of Mr. Loveland's second daughter, Miss Fanny Vaughn
Loveland to Robert Packer Brodhead of Flemington, New Jersey.
The ceremony was performed by the Rev. F. von Krug after the
ritual of the Presbyterian church. The bride's costume was of
heavy corded silk, en train, trimmed with Duchess lace. She wore
diamond ornaments. The groom wore the usual evening dress.
During the ceremony, Oppenheimer's full string orchestra of
Wilkes Barre, played the wedding march. The guests only included the relatives of the contracting parties and a few intimate
friends. After an elaborate spread the young couple left amid
showers of rice, to take the late afternoon train on the L. V. R. R.
The tour will occupy about three weeks, after which the young
couple will live in Flemington, N. J., where the groom holds a
position under the Lehigh Valley R. R. The wedding presents
quite filled a spacious room. There were included a glittering and
costly set of silverware, cut-glass, bric-a-brac, and other beautiful
remembrances.—Wilkes Barre Record, Thursday, May 23, 1889.

Author's Impression of The Ladies

Homemakers

The ladies who contributed to *RECIPES* represented the
middle and upper-income classes of 1907 Kingston.
Compared to their immigrant neighbors, the ladies were
quite economically and educationally advantaged.
Consider that 43% of the ladies retained live-in household
servants. This rate is more than twice the national
percentage of that period. In addition, it is likely that some
of the ladies had part-time servants to help them during
the day. In the early 1900s, extended families were the
norm rather than the exception, so in some homes, family
members helped with housekeeping chores and child
rearing.

Because of their advantages, the ladies were not totally consumed by the home and family. Socially, they were able to participate in church activities and projects like *RECIPES*, to lead organizations such as the Visiting Nurses Association, and to organize social events including: cotillions, dress soirees, beautiful wedding celebrations, balls, masquerades, concerts, art lectures, and private parties. Civically, they were able to advocate for and to create governmental and social reform. Parentally, they were able to provide educational opportunity for their children. At the same time, they maintained the supremacy of their primary role as daughter, sister, wife, mother and keeper of the home.

Activists

Like their counterparts nationwide, the ladies of the Kingston Presbyterian Church were leaders of Progressive Era reform in their community. For example, four of the ladies, Mrs. R. P. (Fannie) Brodhead, Miss Elizabeth Loveland, Mrs. M. E. (Bertha) Marvin, and Mrs. Andrew Raub were among a group of twelve women who, in 1903, began the Women's Civic Club, which was the beginning of today's Wyoming Valley Women's Club.

By 1908, the club was working with the Wilkes-Barre City council, the board of trade, and the mayor to improve "general hygiene, schools, and the city streets." In 1910, the club became part of the national organization and regular meetings were held at the Wilkes-Barre YWCA. Annual dues were $1 and there were approximately 130 active members. A true Progressive Era organization, the club's mission was "To arouse civic consciousness to the need of preserving the natural beauty of the city, and to awaken a latent sense of civic responsibility." [18]

Nativists (?)[19]

The growth of the Anthracite coal industry and the unprecedented influx of immigrants speaking a variety of languages and bringing new traditions from the "old country" made life both exciting and stressful for the residents of Kingston in 1907. Numerically, the "foreigners" were overwhelming and intimidating to the native born population. Immigrants were feared and held in distain by nativists who were concerned with maintaining the purity of what they claimed to be the Anglo-Saxon race. Immigrants were widely assaulted by nativist intellectuals in newspapers, books, and lectures. As well as in some Sunday sermons in the Protestant churches.

Unfortunately, we can only guess about the individual attitudes and reactions of the ladies. But, similar to today, there must have been palpable differences in their response to these great changes. Some, like their contemporary Wilkes-Barre activist Miss Edith Brower, recognized the immigrant's troubles and taught them English to help improve their situation. However, many others were surely convinced that all they valued was being destroyed by the large influx of legal immigrants otherwise known as "foreigners."

Anne Roller, a social worker of the period, described the situation in the following manner:

> "To the townsfolk, especially to the families who go back for generations…, the miners are foreigners, Polaks Wops, "the men in the mines." They are appalled that the foreigners now so far outnumber the native stock. They realize that the hazardous work of mining must be done, but they resent the demands of the men who do it for higher wages and better living conditions. In its extreme, this feeling takes the form that the foreign miners are a lower order of beings; they may be blamed for "living like pigs" and at the same time censured for every strike much is made of the fact that some miners own automobiles and houses; the implication being that they are a presumptuous and unreasonable lot."[20]

In Kingston, as in most communities, the "foreigners" and the established residents, who were the shopkeepers, bankers, railroad clerks, and physicians, did not mingle. The *RECIPES* cookbook and the 96 ladies provide us with some evidence that the community was not a "melting pot." With few exceptions, the ladies represented families long established in the Kingston community. Some of the ladies could trace their ancestry to pre-Revolutionary times. As noted earlier, in 1907 over 60% of Kingston's population was foreign born or had at least one parent who was foreign born. However, not one of the ladies who contributed to *RECIPES* had a southern or eastern European surname. In addition, *RECIPES* does not include a single recipe representing the new immigrants. Today, it is hard to imagine life in Kingston without Irish stew, spaghetti sauce, Hungarian goulash, pierogies or halusky.

The separateness was endemic and affected all aspects of community life. Even the local social agencies faced difficulties in meeting the needs of the immigrants. Raising funds to support charitable activities is always difficult, but in this period providing services to immigrant families was made more problematic by the nativist mindset many volunteers and donors brought to the situation. Social worker, Anne Roller, wrote the following to describe the predominant thinking of volunteers and donors:

> *"One of the local children's agencies a year or two ago made up Christmas packages for its wards. All of the girls within a certain age group were given warm soft wooly scarfs. There were grey scarfs with black stripes and there were gay ones of red, blue and green. Apparently unconscious of the incongruity of their choice, the committee sent the dull-colored ones to the foreign girls! The agencies which supply gifts to the needy at Christmas find it difficult to distribute*

the generous donations that pour in, because of the string so
often tied to the gift..."For a nice American family."[21]

Reformers saw their challenge as molding the new immigrants into orderly and educated Americans. Children of the immigrants were the main targets of their efforts. With the focus on children, efforts naturally turned to the schools to lead the "Americanization" of the immigrants. In their best light, public schools fostered, nurtured, and cultivated the immigrant children into productive American citizens. At their worst, the schools were seen as culturally biased agents determined to destroy immigrant families, beliefs and traditions.

However, today's residents of Kingston and Luzerne County look back and see the positive value of the ethnic diversity that is their heritage. This attitude is evident from the following statement on the current Luzerne County website:

A Diverse and Dynamic Culture[22]

"Because of the immigrants that made this valley their home during this great period of American immigration, Luzerne County has an incredibly rich and diverse culture. The churches, neighborhoods, schools, gathering places, restaurants, and taverns located throughout this county are a lasting testament to the rich mixture of immigration that came into this beautiful valley. For more than a century, those diverse cultures mixed, inter-married, and merged to create a community that has a unique sense of place; a place that began with coal mining, railroading, and manufacturing, and is now a place that is keenly aware of its heritage and the essential reasons for preserving that heritage."

Part Four: *RECIPES* Review and Instructions

Book Club Review

In May 2012, the members of Church of Christ Uniting's Lunch Bunch Book Club reviewed *RECIPES*. The club members marveled at the difficulty of food preparation and preservation without electric refrigeration, especially considering that numerous recipes called for the use of butter, milk, and lard. They expressed concern about the threat of food borne illnesses, noting that diarrhea was among the five leading causes of illness and death in the early 1900s. Another concern was the disproportionate high number of recipes for deserts, jams, and candies. Nearly 50% of the 450 recipes are for desserts. The club members expressed their understanding that the cooks of 1907 were not aware of the connection of diet to illness such as cardiovascular disease. However, the book club members cautioned that a steady diet drawn from *RECIPES* regardless of how tasty could be a "Diet for Death!"

Instructions for Cooking the Recipes[23]

To get the same results as the ladies of the Kingston Presbyterian Church you will need to use period ingredients like real butter, cream, lard and so on. Otherwise, they will not taste the same and some may not work at all. Old recipes were designed for use with unbleached flour and often will not work with bleached flour because of additives and bleaching agents that cause the flour to act differently. Historic recipes will not taste the same and may not work properly when you substitute modern ingredients for the use of lard in cooking. In addition, the recipes were originally cooked on a coal stove or, perhaps, even an open hearth.

Measurements

Old recipes used different units of measurement than we do today. Standardized measurements did not appear until the late 1890's. Where teaspoons or tablespoons are mentioned they are the spoons used to eat and serve food. A cup meant a teacup and a glass or tumbler was a small water glass. The following table gives the modern equivalents for the period measurement used in the recipes.

Liquids
1 pint = 16 ounces or 2 cups
1 pint of liquid = 1 pound
1 gill = 1/2 cup or 4 ounces
1/2 gill = 1/4 cup or 2 ounces
1 kitchen cup = 1 cup or 8 ounces
1 tumbler = 1 cup or 8 ounces
16 Tablespoons liquid = 1 cup
1 wineglass = 1/2 cup or 4 ounces
1 tablespoon = 1/2 ounce
4 teaspoons = 1 tablespoon
salt spoon = 1/4 teaspoon
60 drops = 1 teaspoon

Dry Ingredients
1 heaping quart of sifted flour = 1 pound
4 cups flour = 1 pound or 1 quart
3 cups cornmeal = 1 pound
1 1/2 pints cornmeal = 1 pound
1 pint white sugar = 2 cups or 1 pound
1 pint brown sugar = 13 ounces
2 1/2 cups powdered sugar = 1 pound
1 rounded tablespoon flour = 1/2 ounce, or one modern tablespoon

Miscellaneous
1 egg = 1 medium egg
10 eggs (or 9 large eggs) = 1 pound
1 solid pint of chopped meat = 1 pound
A dash = 3 good shakes
A pottle = 2 quarts or 4 pounds
1 peck = 8 quarts or 2 gallons

1 bushel = 4 pecks or 8 gallons
1 tablespoon butter = 1 ounce
1 pint butter = 2 cups or 1 pound
1 cup butter = 1/2 pound or 8 ounces
Butter the size of a hickory nut = 1 heaping teaspoon or 1/2 ounce
Butter the size of a walnut = 2 heaping teaspoons or 1 ounce
Butter the size of an egg = 1/3 cup or 2 ounces
Butter the size of a turkey or goose egg = 3/4 stick, 3/8 cup, or 3 ounces
1 package yeast = 2 teaspoons"

Other Cooking Challenges

While the foregoing information is helpful, readers are forewarned of other challenges to preparing these recipes. For instance, often the recipes are simply a list of ingredients without instructions. Cooking times and temperatures are a more modern invention and a recipe like the one for Beaf Loaf tells us to "Bake an hour and a quarter" but is silent as to the oven temperature. On the other hand, the recipe for Oyster Pie says to "bake in a quick oven" without mention to how long to bake the pie. Or, for that matter what a "quick oven" means. Other instructions like "cook until done" or "milk to make a batter" may also challenge readers aspiring to cook like their grandmother and/or great grandmother.

Encouragement from Miss Elizabeth Loveland

It is a reasonable guess that Miss Elizabeth Loveland led the creation and publication of *RECIPES*. The niece of a former governor, in 1907 she was a 43 year old independently wealthy unmarried woman who led by example collecting 25 recipes. As the leader of the ladies, Miss Loveland would be certain to advise you…not to worry about the cooking challenges. Just start cooking and enjoying a bit of the lives, times and recipes of the ladies of the Kingston Presbyterian Church!

Part Five: *RECIPES*

Soups

Clam Chowder—Maryland Style.
½ Lb. Fat Salt Pork.
Salt, Pepper.
6 Chopped Onions.
25 Clams.
1 Qt. Tomatoes.
1 Doz. Chopped Potatoes.
1 Tablespoon Worcestershire Sauce
Pinch Of Thyme.
1 Qt. Oysters.

Chop Pork, Brown In Frying Pan. Remove Hard Part Of Clams, Chop Fine. Boil Clams, Onions, Pork, Tomatoes And Seasoning Four Hours With One Pint Water And Juice Of Clams. Add Potatoes Three Quarters Hour Before Serving; And Clams Ten Minutes Before.

Mrs. R. B Vaughn.

Corn Chowder.
1 Qt. Cabbage. 1 Qt. Green Tomatoes.
1 Qt. Corn. 1 Qt. Celery.
1 Qt. Lima Beans. 3 Qts. Vinegar.
1 Qt Green Cucumbers. 1 Oz. Mustard Seed.
1 Qt. Green, Red And
2 Lbs. Sugar Yellow Peppers.

Boil One-Half Hour. Do Not Put Corn In Until Fifteen Minutes Before Removing From Fire.

Mrs. M. A. Van Scoy.

Vegetable Soup Stock.

1 Bushel Tomatoes.   ½ Peck Onions
1 Peck Okra.   10 Green Peppers.
2 Red Peppers.   1 Cup Salt.
   If Desired, Add 1 Doz. Large Or 2 Doz.
Small Ears Of Corn.   Scald, Skin, Squeeze
And Stew Tomatoes As For Table Use. Add
Onions And Peppers Skinned And Free From
Seeds And Chopped. When Cooked Add
Okra Cut In Discs. Stir Frequently, Add Salt,
And When Okra Is Tender, Put Into Glass
Jars And Seal. One Pint Thickens One Quart
Of Meat Stock.

Mrs. Andrew Raub.

Bean Soup.

1 Pt. Cold Baked Beans. 1 Teaspoon Butter.
1 Qt. Water.   1 Teaspoon Flour.
½ Tea Cup Catsup.
   Put The Beans Over The Fire In The Water
And When Soft Rub Through A Colander.
Return To The Fire, Add The Catsup, And
Salt And Pepper, If Needed. Rub The Butter
And Flour Together And Stir Into The Soup.
Boil. Serve With Croutons Or Bread Browned
Slightly In Oven.

Mrs. R. P.
Brodhead.

Chicken Soup.

1 Qt. Chicken Broth.
1 Tablespoon Chopped Parsley
3 Cups Milk Or Cream
1 Teaspoon Salt.
¼ Cup Chopped Celery.
Dash Of Cayenne.
½ Tablespoon Butter.
1 Tablespoon Flour.
   Rub Butter And Flour Together Before
Using. Add Some Hot Stock And Stir Until

Smooth, Then Stir Into Soup. Boil Up Once
And Serve.

Mrs. W. H. Faulds.

Cream Of Pea Soup.

One Pt. Peas Boiled And Mashed Through
A Colander. Place In A Sauce Pan One
Tablespoon Butter; When Melted, Add 2 Even
Tablespoons Flour. Stir Well And Add Slowly
1 Pt. Boiling Water, 1 Qt. Boiling Milk, Then
Mashed Peas. Cook Until Blended. Season
With Salt And Pepper. Serve Very Hot.

Mrs. B. R. Tubbs.

Tomato Puree.

1 Qt. Canned Or Fresh Tomatoes.
Sprig Of Parsley.
Stick Of Celery,
1 Pt. Water Or Stock Preferred
6 Pepper Corns.
1 Bay Leaf
1 Teaspoon Sugar.

Put In Granite Ware Sauce Pan. Simmer
Until Tomato Is Soft. In Another Sauce Pan
Fry A Sliced Onion And Tablespoon Butter.
Add Tablespoon Flour And Cook But Not
Brown. Add Enough Tomato To Dilute
Mixture. Mix Well With Rest Of Tomato And
Salt. Strain. Heat Again Before Serving.
Serve With Croutons.

Mrs. C. W. Bixby.

Black Bean Soup.

L Pt. Black Turtle Soup Beans
½ Lb. Beef Bone.
1 Carrot Cut Or Grated
1 Onion
1 Turnip
1 Teaspoon Whole Cloves Or Allspice

Soak Beans Over Night. Put Beans Into Six Quarts Cold Water With Other Ingredients And Boil Three Or Four Hours. Put Through Colander, Add Thickening And Boil A Few Minutes Longer. Add Wine. Put Slices Of Lemon And Hard Boiled Eggs In Tureen And Pour Soup Over.

Mrs. H. H. Welles, Jr.

Potato Soup.

Cut A Small Portion, Salt Bacon In Small Pieces And Boil Twenty Minutes With A Few Slices Of Onion. When Bacon Is Nearly Done Add Two Potatoes, And Boil Until Done. Remove Potatoes, Mash Them And Put Them Back In The Saucepan, Adding One Tablespoon Butter, One Cup Milk, One Teaspoon Cornstarch. Season.

Mrs. C. Bach.

Fish

Oyster Cocktail.

5 Small Oysters To A Glass.

1/2 Teaspoon Tabasco Sauce.

I Cup Oyster Liquor.   Juice Of Lemon.

L/2 Cup Catsup.   Salt

Mrs. T. L. Welles.

Oyster Pie.

Line Deep Pie Plate With Pie Crust And Fill With Two Layers Of Oysters Putting On Each Layer Flour, Pepper, Salt And A

Piece Of Butter. Cover With Upper Crust And
Bake In Quick Oven.

Mrs. C. Bach.

Fricasee Of Oysters.

Boil Twenty-Five Oysters In Their
Own Liquor And Drain In A Colander. Cook
One Minute In A Sauce Pan. Stirring All The
Time.
Butter Size Of Egg.
1 Tablespoon Flour.
1 Cup Oyster Liquor.
Take From Fire And Mix In Yolks Of Two
Eggs Or The Whole Eggs. Add Salt. Cayenne
Pepper. 1 Teaspoon Lemon Juice And A
Grating Of Nutmeg. Return To Fire To Set
The Eggs, Put In Oysters To Heat And Serve
On Thin Slices Of Toast Or In Patty Shells.

Mrs. B. R. Tubbs.

A Nice Dish For Tea.

One Pint Stewing Oysters Chopped Quite
Fine, 1 Egg Well Beaten.
Add A Handful Coarse Cracker Crumbs Salt
And Pepper To Taste. Drop By Spoonfuls In
Hot Butter And Fry A Nice Brown.

Mrs. Cooper.

Creamed Oysters.

25 Oysters.

1 Tablespoon Corn Starch Or Flour.
1 Pt. Cream.
1 Tablespoon Butter.
Mace, Salt, Pepper.
Boil Oysters In Their Own Liquor And
Drain Through Colander. Cook Cream, Etc.,

In Double Boiler. Add Oysters, Stir Until
Thoroughly Heated And Serve.

Mrs. B. R. Tubbs.

Lobster Newberg.

Split / Two Good Sized Freshly Boiled Lobsters.
Pick Meat From Shells And Cut Into Inch Long
Pieces. Place Them In Sauce Pan On Hot Range
With One Tablespoon Butter. Season With One
Large Pinch Of Salt And Same Amount Of Red
Pepper. Cook Five Minutes Then Add One
Wineglass Of Madeira Or Sherry Wine. Boil Three
Minutes And Set Aside. Beat Yolks Of Three Eggs
Light, Add To Them 1/2 Pint Sweet Cream, And A
Cup Of Sweet Milk. Put The Whole In A Separate
Sauce Pan And Heat Very Hot. Stir Into It A
Teaspoon Of Cornstarch Which Has Been Dissolved
In Cold Water, And Add The Mixture To The
Lobster. Turn Into Hot Tureen And Serve On Hot
Plates.

Miss Augusta Hoyt.

Rock Fish Or Halibut A La Creme.

Boil The Fish In Salted Water. When Done
Remove The Skin And Take Out The Bone.   (This Is
For Rock.) Make A Dressing With 1 Pint Of Milk
And 1 Pint Of Cream, Butter The Size Of An Egg
And Three Tablespoons Of Flour, Adding A Little
Chopped Parsley, Half A Chopped Onion, Salt And
Pepper.
Stir This On The Fire Until Thick, Take From Fire
And Thoroughly Cool. Butter A Dish And Put In
Alternate Layers Of Fish And Dressing, Sprinkling
The Fish With A Thin Layer Of Grated Cheese. The
Dressing Must Be The Top Layer. Sprinkle With
Bread Crumbs, Cheese And Small Bits Of Butter.
Bake 30 Minutes.

Miss Augusta Hoyt.

Salmon Balls.

1 Can Salmon.	1/2 Cup Milk.
2 Eggs.	1 Cup Cracker Crumbs.
Fry In Hot Fat.	

Mrs. Hilbert

Salmom Cakes.

1 Can Salmon.
½ Cup Bread Or Cracker Crumbs
1 Egg.
½ Cup Milk.
¼ Teaspoon Baking Powder
1/2 Teaspoon Salt.

Beat Eggs And Salmon Together Until Smooth. Add Other Ingrediants And Drop From Spoon Into Hot Lard And Butter.

J. A. S.

Escolloped Salmon.

2 Cups Milk.	Yolks Of Two Eggs.
2 Tablespoons Flour.	

Cook Together And When Thick Add Beaten Whites Of Eggs. Arrange Layers Of Salmon, Bread Crumbs, Bits Of Butter And The Above Dressing. Bake One-Half Hour In Buttered Dish.

S. S. Goodwin

Oyster Cocktail.

Eight Tablespoons Tomato Catsup, Six Tablespoons Of Lemon Juice, One Tablespoon Of Worcestershire Sauce, One Tablespoon Grated Horseradish, One Salt Spoon Of Salt, Six Drops Of Tobasco Sauce. Mix Together And Keep Very Cool

Until Ready To Serve. Put The Oysters Into Punch Glasses And Fill With The Mixture.
This Is Sufficient For Eight Glasses.

Mrs. M. E. Marvin

Meats

Oatmeal Stuffing.

Cook One Heaping Cup Of Irish Or Scotch Oatmeal In A Double Boiler, With Salt, Pepper, A Medium Onion, Two Cold Sausages Chopped Fine And Piece Of Butter Size Of An Egg. A Slice Of Pork May Be Used In Place Of Sausage. Pourover This Boiling Water Enough To Cover Mixture. Let This Stand Over The Fire Until Water Is All Taken Up By Oatmeal. It Need Not Boil Hard All The Time. Do Not Stuff Breast Of Turkey Too Full. It Is Necessary That The Right Amount Of Water Be Used. The Dressing Should Be Almost Crumbling When Served.

Miss Elizabeth Loveland.

Baked Meat Dish.

Put Layer Of Chopped Beef Or Veal In Baking Dish, Then Layer Of Raw Canned Tomatoes, Seasoned, And Then Layer Of Cooked Vermicelli. Repeat. Cover With Bread Crumbs And Lumps Of Butter. Gravy Adds To It. Bake One And One-Half Hours.

Miss Katharine Parsons.

Potted Or Jellied Meat.—Scotch Dish.

A Shin Of Beef, Broken For Boiling. Cover With Cold Water And Boil Until Meat Comes From Bone.

54

Cool, Skim, Cut Meat Fine And Replace In Kettle After Straining Liquor. Season And Boil Briskly For Half An Hour. Put In Molds And Keep In Cool Place.

Mrs. Duncan Stewart.

Yorkshire Pudding.

5 Tablespoons Flour.   2 Eggs.
1 Pt. Sweet Milk. Salt.
   Beat Flour And Milk; Add Eggs Well Beaten And Salt. Bake In Meat Gravy After Removing Roast. Bake In Hot Oven Twenty-Five Minutes.

Mrs. R. B. Vaughn.

Baked Ham.

One Slice Ham One-Half Inch Thick. Place In Skillet With A Little Water. Sprinkle Ham With A Little Sugar. Hake One Hour.

Mrs. Benner.

Baked Cured Ham.

Soak A Ham Over Night. In The Morning Put On To Boil In Cold Water. Let It Simmer Two Or Three Hours. Let Ham Remain In Kettle Until Luke Warm. Remove Skin And Bake In Oven For Two Hours, Using Cup Of Wine, Vinegar Or Hard Cider Sweetened With Brown Sugar To Baste With. Baste Frequently.
When Baked, Spread Ham With A Paste Made Of Fine Bread Crumbs, Two Teaspoons Brown Sugar, One Teaspoon Dry Mustard, Moistened With Cider Or Wine. Return Ham To Oven Long Enough To Brown Well.

Mrs. B. R. Tubbs.

Sausage.
100 Lbs. of 1/2 Lean And ½ Half Fat Meat Chopped Fine.

10 Oz. Ground Sage.

10 Oz. Black Pepper.

2 ½ Lbs. Salt.

Mix Meat And Seasoning Thoroughly. Keep In Cool Place.

Miss Frances Dorrance.

Farmer's Dainty Dish.
5 Potatoes

1 Onion

½ Lb. Salt Pork, Sliced.

1 Lb. Beef, Mutton-Or Veal.

Peel And Slice Thin The Potatoes And Onion. Cut Meat In Small Pieces. Shorten Bread Or Biscuit Dough. In A Stew Pan Place Slices Of Pork, Meat, Potato And Onion, A Little Pepper, Then A Layer Of Crust. Repeat This Until The Stew Pot Is Full. Pour In Water To Cover And Finish With Crust. Simmer Until All Is Done, But Do Not Let Boil. Serve Hot.

Mrs. Andrew Raub.

Beaf Loaf
3 Lbs. Chopped Beef.

2 Eggs.

4 Crackers, Rolled.

Butter Size Of Egg.

1 Tablespoon Of Salt.

1 Teaspoon Pepper.

½ Nutmeg, Grated.

½ Cup Of Milk.

Bake An Hour And A Quarter.

Mrs. Albert E. Miller

Spring Chicken.
Open Chickens Down Back And Spread Out. Rub The Whole Chicken With Butter, Then Sprinkle In Mustard And Salt. Roast About One Hour, Basting

56

Frequently. Have Very Little Water In The Pan.
Make A Little Gravy And Pour Over.

Miss Katharine Parsons.

Chicken And Macaroni.

One Cup Macaroni Broken And Boiled In Salted Water. Pick Up Stewed Chicken. Place Layers Of Chicken And Macaroni In Dish, Sprinkle On Top Cracker Or Bread Crumbs And Bits Of Butter. Pour On The Layers A Dressing Of Two Tablespoons Melted Butter And Two Tablespoons Flour, One Pint Boiling Milk And One Cup Liquor From Chicken. Season.

Mrs. James H. Hughes.

Savory Meat

3 Lbs. Round Steak.
1/2 Tablespoon Salt.
Ground.
1 Teaspoon Of Pepper.
  Bake In Loaf.

3 Eggs.
6 Crackers,

Butter.

Mrs. C. Bach.

Corned Beef—Quick Made.

5 Lbs. Beef.
Saltpetre Size Hazle Nut.
Sugar.

4 Teaspoons Salt.
2 Tablespoons

Dissolve Salt, Sugar And Saltpetre In Enough Water To Cover Beef. Let Stand Two Or Three Days, And Boil Tender In The Same Water. Skim While Boiling.

Roasted Veal Cutlets.

Sprinkle Cutlets With Salt And Pepper. Dip In Egg And Bread Crumbs.

Put Bits Of Butter On Cutlets, And Put In Pan With
One Cup Water.   Roast In Hot Oven.

Mrs. F. W. Frantz.

Veal Loaf. No. 1.

3 Lbs. Veal, Chopped Fine.

2 Teaspoons Summer Savory

½ Cup Bread Or Cracker Crumbs.

½ Lb. Beef, Chopped Fine.

½ Teaspoon Allspice.

2 Teaspoons Salt.

3 Eggs.

3 Tablespoons Cream.

1 Teaspoon Black Pepper.

1/2 Cup Butter.

1 Teaspoon Onion Juice.

   Mix The Meat, Crumbs And Seasoning, Add Eggs,
Well Beaten, Cream And Melted Butter. Press Into A
Mould Wet With Cold Water, Then Turn Out On A
Flat Baking Pan. Bake In Moderate Oven Two
Hours, Basting Occasionally With Melted Butter.

Mrs. D. H. Lake.

Veal Loaf. No. 2.

2 Lbs. Veal, Chopped.

2 Eggs.

¼ Lb. Salt Pork, Chopped.

Butter Size Of Egg.

1 ½ Tablespoons Cream.

Salt, Pepper.

½ Nutmeg.

A Little Parsley.

½ Cup Bread Crumbs.

   Bake One And One-Half Hours.

Mrs. T. W. Thomas.

Veal Loaf. No. 3.

3 Lbs. Raw Chopped Veal.

6 Soda Crackers, Rolled.

3 Beaten Eggs.

1 Tablespoon Salt.

I Teaspoon Pepper.

A Little Summer Savory.

   Mix And Make Into A Round, Long Loaf. Bake Two And One-Half Hours, Basting Every Fifteen Minutes With The Butter And Water In Pan.

Miss Katharine Parsons,
Miss Hasseby.

Veal Loaf. No. 4.
1/4 Lb. Salt Pork, Chopped.
4 Tablespoons Melted Butter
2 Lbs. Veal, Chopped Fine.
½ Cup Cracker Crumbs.
Salt And Pepper.
3 Eggs.
A Little Onion Juice.

Mrs. Philip Hessel.

Vegetables

Escolloped Tomatoes.
   Season A Can Of Tomatoes With 1 Teaspoon Salt And 1/4 Teaspoon Pepper. Spread A Shallow Baking Dish With Thin Layer Of Bread Crumbs ; Pour In The Tomatoes, Sprinkle Over Them 1 Teaspoon Sugar; Cover The Top With A Cupful Of Bread Crumbs Which Has Been Moistened With A Tablespoon Of Melted Butter.   Bake In Hot Oven 15 Minutes.

Miss Esther French.

Spanish Spaghetti.

Break One-Half Pound Spaghetti Into Small Pieces, Cover With Boiling Water And Boil Twenty Minutes. Slice One Medium Sized Onion And Fry Slightly Brown In Butter; Add Three Or Four Large Tomatoes, Or Half A Can Of Tomatoes, Half Dozen Or More Chilies And Salt. Cook All Together, Then Strain, If Desired, Before Adding Spaghetti. Cook With The Tomato Sauce A Few Minutes Longer.

Mrs. H. B. Payne.

Macaroni.

When Macaroni Is Well Cooked Add Butter Size Of An Egg, Salt, Pepper, Tablespoon Mustard Mixed With Vinegar. Grate Cheese. Cover With Milk And Bread Crumbs.

Mrs. B. R. Tubbs.

Potato Fritters.

2 Cups Mashed Potato. Salt. Pepper.
2 Eggs, Unbeaten.   Flour To Make Thick Batter.
1 Teaspoon Baking Powder.
  Fry In Hot Lard.

Mrs. F. W. Frantz

Stuffed Tomatoes.

1 Tablespoon Melted Butter.
1 Heaping Cup Of Bread Crumbs
1 Tablespoon Onion, Chopped.
1 Teaspoon Of Salt
1 Cup Minced Meat (Chicken Or Lamb).
Dash Of Pepper.
1 Tablespoon Chopped Parsley.
Pulp Of Tomatoes

Fry Onion And Butter Together, Add Other Ingredients And Stir Over Fire Until Of Right Consistency. Cut Slice From End Of Tomato And Remove Inside. Rub Inside With Onion. Fill With Stuffing. Place Small Lump Of Butter On Top. Place

Each Tomato On Piece Of Toast Well Moistened.
Bake Fifteen Minutes. Serve With Brown Sauce.
Mrs. D. H. Lake.

Cucumbers.
Slice Together, Very Thin, 4 Or 5 Cucumbers And
1 Small Onion. Sprinkle With Salt And Let Stand
Half An Hour. Wring Out With The Hands. Cover
With ¾ Cup Of Thick Cream Mixed With 1/4 Cup
Vinegar. Sprinkle With Pepper.
Mrs. John E. Jenkins.

Baked Beans.
At Noon Put To Soak One Quart Beans; At Night
Drain, Put In Baking Dish, Adding One Pound Salt
Bacon, Two Tablespoons Sugar, One Tablespoon
Mustard And Pinch Of Cayenne. Cover Beans With
Water And Bake Until Morning.
Mrs. M. A. Scureman.

Dry Fried Onions
Peel And Slice White Bermuda Or Spanish Onions.
Allow To Separate Into Rings. Soak In Sweet Milk
For Ten Minutes. Sprinkle A Little Flour On-Bread
Board. Drain Onions And Place On Board.
Sprinkle Lightly With Flour, Fry In Hot Lard, As
Potato Chips.
Drain, Salt To Taste. Cover Platter With Napkin
And Serve.
Mrs. F. L. Olds.

Stuffed Egg-Plant.
Boil An Egg-Plant Thirty Minutes. Cut In Half,
Scrape Out The Inside. Mash This With Two
Tablespoons Butter, Season With Salt And Pepper.
Fill The Halves With The Pulp, Sprinkle With Bread
Crumbs And Brown In Oven. A Little Minced Veal
Or Chicken May Be Added To The Pulp.
Miss Frances Dorrance.

Peas, Martinique Style.

1 Tablespoon Olive Oil.	1 Tablespoon Batter,
I Can Peas.	1 Onion, Medium.
Sugar.	Salt.

Put Oil And Butter In Pan ; When Hot, Add Peas, From Which Liquid Has Been Drained, The Onion Grated, Salt And Sugar. Heat And Serve.

Mrs. L. C. Darte.

Potato Snow.

Boil Large Potatoes In Skins, Drain And Dry Thoroughly. Peel. Heat A Dish, And Rub Potatoes Through A Coarse Sieve Into This Dish. Do Not Touch Them Afterward Or The Flakes Will Fall. Serve Very Hot.

Miss Lawley.

Hashed Brown Potatoes.

2 Tablespoons Butter.
1 Qt. Cold Boiled Potatoes.
Salt And Pepper.

Put Butter In Spider, When Melted, Add Potatoes Coarsely Hashed. Season. Press Lightly With Back Of Spoon, Cover And Brown For Fifteen Minutes. Turn Out As An Omelet.

Miss Esther French.

Entrees

Welsh Rarebit.

1 Tablespoon Butter.	Red Pepper.
2 Bs. Cheese, Grated Or Cut.	Salt.
1 Egg.	1 Small Cup
Cream.	
Mustard.	

Melt Together Butter And Cheese. When Nearly
Melted Add Mustard, Red Pepper And Salt. When
Smooth, Add Yolk Of Egg And Cream. Stir A Few
Minutes. Add Beaten White Of Egg.

Union League Club.

Egg Cutlets.
3 Hard Boiled Eggs, Chopped
1 Teaspoon Chopped Parsley
1 Cup Of Milk.
1 Tablespoon Onion Juice.
1 Tablespoon Flour.
Black Pepper.
1 Tablespoon Melted Butter.

Heat Milk In Double Boiler; Stir Into It Flour And
Butter, Stirring Until Smooth. Add Parsley, Onion
Juice And Pepper To Eggs And Cook A Few Minutes
With Milk In Double Boiler.   Turn Out On Platter
To Cool. Form Into Cutlets, Dip In Egg, Then In
Bread Crumbs And Fry In Hot Fat. Stick A Sprig Of
Parsley In Each Cutlet Before Serving. Pour Over
Them A Cream Sauce Made With
2 Tablespoons Butter.
1 Pt. Milk Seasoned With Salt And Pepper.
2 Tablespoons Flour.

When Boiling Add Half-Pint Of Cooked Peas To
The Sauce.

Miss Augusta Hoyt.

Liver Terrapin.
½ A Calf's Liver
2 Tablespoons Butter.
1/2 Pt. Water.
1 Gill Wine.
1 Tablespoon Mustard.
1 Pinch Cayenne.
2 Hard Boiled Eggs, Chopped.

Boil Or Fry Liver, Then Cut Into Dice. Melt Butter,
Stir In Flour, Add A Little Water, Then The Liver To

63

Which The Dry Seasoning Has Been Added. Add
Wine And Eggs When The Mixture Boils Up.   Serve
At Once.

Mrs. B. R. Tubbs.

Chicken Souffle.

1 Tablespoon Butter.

1 Tablespoon Flour.

1 Tablespoon Parsley, Chopped

1 Cup Milk.

1 Cup Minced Chicken.

3 Eggs.

Dash Pepper.   ½ Teaspoon
Salt.

Make White Sauce Of The Butter, Flour, Milk And
Seasoning. Remove From Fire And Stir In The
Beaten Yolks And The Chicken. Stir Mixture Over
The Fire A Minute, Then Set Aside To Cool, Just
Before Serving Stir The Beaten Whites Into The
Chicken, And Bake In A Hot Oven Twenty Minutes.
Veal Or Lamb May Be Used.

Miss Elizabeth Loveland.

Cheese Souffle.

3 Eggs, Well Beaten.

2 Tablespoons Butter.

1 Cup Mild Cheese, Grated.

1 Tablespoon Flour.

1/2 Teaspoon Salt.

1/2 Cup Milk.

Dash Of Red Pepper.

Bake Twenty Minutes In Buttered Dish.

Mrs. J. D. Flanagan.

Cucumber Aspic.

4 Large Cucumbers.

Salt And White Pepper To Taste.

1 Small Onion. Taste.

½ A Box Gelatine Soaked In ½ Cup Cold Water.

Peel Cucumbers And Cut In Thick Slices. Put Them And The Sliced Onion Over The Fire With A Scant Quart Of Water. Simmer For An Hour, Stir In The Gelatine, And When This Is Dissolved, Season The Jelly. Strain And Turn Into Moulds Or Glasses.

Cheese Balls.
1/2 Cup Grated Cheese.
1/2 Teaspoon Salt.
¼ Teaspoon Red Pepper.
Yolks Of Two Eggs.
 Mix Thoroughly, Make Balls, Roll In Fine Bread Crumbs, Then In Beaten Egg Several Times And Cook In Hot Oven.

Mrs. Meginess.

Cheese Souffle.
1 Cup Grated Cheese.
1/2 Cup Soft Bread Crumbs,
1 Cup Hot Milk Or Cream.
½ Teaspoon Salt,
1 Tablespoon Butter.
Dash Of Cayenne.
Beaten Yolks Of 3 Eggs.
 Cook All Together Three Minutes, And Then Fold In Whites Of The Three Eggs Beaten Very Stiff. Fill Souffle Dishes Or Big Dish And Bake In Moderate Oven About Fifteen Minutes.

Mrs. C. W. Bixby.

Fried Apples.
 Slice Apples And Take Out Core. Dip In Flour And Fry In Butter. Sprinkle With Sugar And Cinnamon.

Mrs. R. A. Hutchison.

Egg Souffle.
4 Eggs, Yolks And Whites.
1 Tablespoon Butter.

Beaten Separately.
1 1/2 Tablespoons Flour.
1 1/2 Cups Milk.
Salt.

Cook Milk, Flour And Butter Until Smooth, Add Yolks, Take From Fire, Add Whites And Bake 20 Minutes.

Mrs. B. R. Tubbs.

Cheese Fondue.

Four Eggs, The Weight Of Two In Cheese, The Weight Of Two In Butter. Beat The Yolks Of The Eggs, Grate In The Cheese, Or Cut In Thin Flakes, Add The Butter And Plenty Of Red Pepper And Salt. Beat Well, And Then Lightly Stir In The Whites Of The Eggs, Beaten Stiff. Bake In A Small Round Dish, Or In Ramekins, And Serve Immediately. Fill The Dish Only Half Full.

Miss Frances Dorrance.

Nuns Toast.

4 Or 5 Hard Boiled Eggs Cut Into Slices.
1 Onion Chopped Fine.
1 Teaspoon Flour.
Butter Half Size Of Egg.
1 Cup Milk.

Cook Onion And Butter Together Without Coloring. Add Flour And Milk, And Stir Until Smooth.   Pour Over Toast.

Mrs. J. G. Sperling.

Corn Oysters.

1 Can Corn Chopped, Or
2 Eggs.
1 Pt. Fresh Sweet Corn
Dash Cayenne And Black Pepper.
2 Heaping Tablespoons Flour.

Beat Eggs Separately. Stir Corn Into Yolks, Add Whites, Beat Gently And Add Seasoning. Drop By Spoonfuls Into Pan Into Two Tablespoons Hot Lard Or Butter. Brown On Both Sides.

Mrs. W. L. Dean

Apple Fritters.

1 Cup Sweet Milk.	¼ Teaspoon Soda.
1/2 Cup Sour Milk.	A Little Salt.
2 Eggs.	Flour.

Batter Not Too Stiff. Apples Sliced Round. Fry In Swimming Lard.

Miss. Esther French.

Corn Fritters.

6 Ears Corn.	A Little Salt And Peper.
2 Eggs.	2 Tablespoons Water.
2 Tablespoons Flour.	

Miss Esther French.

Chicken Souffle.

1/2 Pt. Rich Milk.
1 Tablespoon Chopped Parsley.
2 Tablespoons Butter.
1 Pt. Finely Chopped Chicken Or Turkey.
1 Tablespoon Flour.
½ Cup Bread Crumbs.
Salt.   White Pepper.
Whites Of 4 Eggs Well Beaten.

Mix Flour With Butter And Put With Milk Over Fire. Add Crumbs And Stir To Smooth Paste. Put In Other Ingredients, Cutting The Whites In Last. Bake In Moderate Oven Twenty Minutes Or More, And Serve Very Hot.

Miss Frances Dorrance.

Corn Oysters.

12 Ears Green Corn Grated.   1/2 Teaspoon Salt.
6 Eggs, Yolks And Whites Beaten Separately.

Stir Whites In Last.

Miss Raub.

Chicken Terrapin.
1/2 Pt. Cream.
3 Hard Boiled Eggs (Chopped).
1/4 Lb. Butter.
1 Tablespoon Flour.
Salt.
Cayenne Pepper.
   Rub Butter And Flour Together, Stir Into Cream And Boil. Add Chicken Prepared As For Salad, Eggs, Salt And Pep-Per.   Flavor With Sherry Wine.

Mrs. C. W. Bixby

Bananas Baked.
A—4 Large Bananas, Peeled And Cut In Slices Lengthwise.
         1 Tablespoon Of Melted Butter.
Mix Thoroughly.
 B—   1/4 Cup Sugar.
         1/8 Teaspoon Salt.
         2 Tablespoons Lemon Juice.   2 Tablespoons Of Lemon Juice.
C—1/2 Cup Powdered Macaroons.
         Meringue Of 2 Eggs,
         Whites And Sugar.
   Put A And B In Layers In Baking Dish, Bake Half An Hour: Then Cover With C. Brown Slightly And Serve.

Mrs. C. W. Bixby.

Oatmeal Fritters
1 Cup Cold Cooked Oat-Flake.
1/2 Cup Flour.
2 Eggs.
1/2 Teaspoon Baking Powder.
2 Tablespoons Milk.
   Fry In Hot Fat.

Mrs. Hilbert.

Fried Apples.
Wash And Core Apples. Cut Through In Rings About One Inch Thick. Cook Slowly In Butter And Sugar In Granite Pan Until They Become Almost Clear, Then Brown.

S. S. Goodwin.

Cheese Souffle.
3 Tablespoons Butter.
½ Cup Milk.
3 Tablespoons Flour (Heaping)
3 Eggs, Beaten Separately.
½ Teaspoon Salt, Scant.
1 Cup Grated Cheese.
Dash Cayenne.
Stir Flour Until Smooth With The Butter In A Sauce Pan. Add Yolks, Well Beaten, Milk And Cheese. Cool And Add Whites Of Eggs. Bake In Baking Dish.

Mrs. W. L. Dean.

Rice Fritters.
1/2 Cup Rice, Steamed Until Dry.
1/2 Cup Milk.
1 Heaping Teaspoon Baking.
2 Eggs Beaten Light. Powder.
1 Tablespoon Sugar.
Flour To Thicken. Salt To Taste. Fry In Deep Fat.

Mrs. T. W. Thomas

Oyster Rarebit
Boil Oysters In Their Own Liquor Until Edges Curl. Keep Hot.
1 Tablespoon Salt.
1 Tablespoon Butter.
1 Table Spoon Mustard.
1/ Lb. Grated Cheese.

1 Tablespoon Pepper.

2 Eggs.

Add Oysters To Melted Cheese And Stir In Eggs. Serve On Toast.

Mrs. B. R. Tubbs.

Cheese Balls.

1 Pt. Milk.

Salt And Red Pepper To Taste

1 Teaspoon Butter.

Mix Enough Flour In Milk

1/2 Lb. Grated Cheese.

To Thicken The Mixture.

Heat Milk, Add Other Ingredients And Stir Until Smooth. Pour Out To Cool And Let Stand Several Hours, Or Even Until Next Day. Roll Into Small Balls, Slip The Balls Into Egg And Cracker Crumbs And Fry In Hot Lard.

Mrs. Phillip Hessel.

Chicken Croquettes.

1 Solid Pint Of Finely Chopped Chicken.

1 Tablespoon Lemon Juice,

1 Cup Cream Or Chicken Gravy

3 Tablespoons Butter.

1 Teaspoon onion juice.

1 Tablespoon Flour

4 eggs.

1 Pt. Crumbs To Roll Croquettes

1 Tablespoon

Salt.

1/2 Teaspoon Pepper.

Heat Cream Or Gravy To Boiling Point, Add Flour And Butter Rubbed Together, And As It Thickens Add Seasoning And Chicken. Let Boil Two Minutes And Add Two Eggs Well Beaten. Cool And Form Into Shape With As Little Handling As Possible. Slip Into Beaten Egg, Roll In Bread Crumbs And Fry

One And One-Half Minutes, Or Until Light Brown.
Makes Twelve Medium Sized Croquettes.

Miss Elizabeth Loveland.

Green Corn Fritters.

1 Pt. Grated Corn.	1 Tablespoon Cream.
1 Egg.	1 Tablespoon Flour.
Pinch Salt.	1 Tablespoon Butter,
Melted.	

Beat The Eggs Well, Add Corn, Beat Hard, Add Salt, Butter, Milk And Flour.

Miss Frances Dorrance.

Sweet-Breads Stewed.

Wash, Remove All The Bits Of Skin, Soak In Salt And Water One Hour Then Parboil. Cut Into Small Pieces, Stew In A Little Water Till Tender, Add A Piece Of Butter, A Teaspoon Of Salt, A Teaspoon Of Flour, And Boil Up Once. Serve On Toast Very Hot. May Be Served With Tomato Sauce.

Mrs. M. A. Scureman.

Rosettes.

1 Cup Flour.	1 Teaspoon Lemon Juice,
1 Cup Water.	2 Tablespoons Olive Oil.
Pinch Salt.	

Let Stand One Hour. Time Does Not Hurt.

Mrs. H. C. Smythe.

Karteise Klase.

3 Eggs Beaten.	Grated Rind Of Lemon.
1 Tablespoon Sugar.	2 Cups Milk.
Salt.	

From Biscuit One Day Old Grate The Crust And Cut Each Biscuit In Four Pieces. Dip In Above Mixture, Lay On Plate And Let Stand Two Hours. Roll In The Grated Crust And Fry In Butter. When Fried Roll In Sugar And Cinnamon.

Recipe Is For Twelve Biscuits. They May Be Served With Fruit And Used As A Dessert Or Simply As A Sweet Fritter.

Mrs. L. C Darte.

Cream Croquettes.

A—Boil Together   2 Tablespoons Cornstarch.
1 Pint Milk.   1 Tablespoon Flour.
1 Stick Cinnamon.   Yolks Of 3 Eggs.
B—Beat Together   1/4 Cup Cold Milk.
1/2 Cup Sugar.   1 Saltspoon Salt.

Pour A On B. Stir Well, Strain Into Double Boiler And

Cook Fifteen Minutes, Stirring Often. Add:

1 Teaspoon Butter.   1 Teaspoon Vanilla.

Pour Into Buttered Bread Pan And Cool. When Very Hard, Cut In Strips; Roll In Egg And Crumbs Like A Croquette, And Fry Brown In Hot Lard. Sprinkle With Powdered Sugar And Serve Hot.

Mrs. John E. Jenkins.

Salmon Fritters.

1 Can Salmon.   1/2 Cup Milk,
1 Egg.   A Pinch Of Salt,
1 Cup Of Bread Crumbs.

Fry In Butter.

Mrs. M. Brewster.

Green Corn Omelet.

8 Ears Of Corn, Grated.
1 Tablespoon Butter.
Yolks Of 3 Eggs.
Salt.
1 Pt. Milk.

Beat Whites Of Eggs Stiff And Add Last. Bake In Pudding Dish In Hot Oven, Or Fry In Butter.

Mrs. R. B Vaughn.

Veal Omelet.

3 Lbs. Raw Veal.
Salt And Pepper.
3 Eggs.
3 Boston Crackers Or 6 Small Ones
2 Tablespoons Cream Or Milk.
   Chop Veal, Make Loaf, Spread Over With Butter
And Bake Two Hours, Basting Often.

                         Mrs. C. W.Bixby.

Corn Omelet.
3 Eggs.
1 Cup Milk.3 Ears Corn.
Pepper And Salt,
1 Tablespoon Flour.
   Put In Pan Of Hot Butter And Lard. Brown In
Oven.

                         Mrs. Meginess.

Omelet.
I Cup Sweet Milk.
Salt.
L Tablespoon Flour.
Yolks Of 4 Eggs Well Beaten
   After Mixture Is Well Beaten, Add The Whites
Beaten Stiff.   Fry In Hot Butter And Lard Fifteen
Minutes.

                         Mrs. C. W. Bixby.

Tomato Omelet.
   Break 6 Eggs And Give Them 12 Vigorous Beats,
Or Enough To Break Up Whites And Yolks. Add
Three Tablespoons Milk Or Cream. Dash Of
Pepper. Melt In Frying Pan One Tablespoon Butter.
Do Not Brown. Turn In Eggs, Sprinkle With One
Half Teaspoon Salt. Shake Pan Until Eggs Are Set,
Not Cooked Hard. Take From Fire; Add By
Tablespoons Four Tablespoons Tomatoes Reduced
By Boiling To One-Half Original Bulk. Fold. Loosen
From Edges And Turn Out On Hot Platter.

Miss Augusta Hoyt.

Salads

Oyster Salad.
 Boil Two Dozen Small Oysters Five Minutes In
Water Which Covers Them. Add Little Salt And
Tablespoon Vinegar ; Drain ; Cool. Put Into Salad
Bowl Centre Leaves Of Two Heads Of Lettuce ; Add
Oysters Whole. Pour Over Mayonnaise.   Garnish
With Hard Boiled Eggs.
Mrs. W. L. Stewart.

Banana Salad.
 Dip Halved Bananas Quickly In Lemon Juice. Put
On Lettuce Leaves. Cover With Chopped Pecans
And Mayonnaise Dressing Into Which A Little
Cream Has Been Whipped.
Mrs. C W. Bixby.

Nut Salad.
 One Cup English Walnuts, Chopped Celery, And
Chopped Apples.   Moisten With Any Good Salad
Dressing.
Mrs. R. B Vaughn.

Cabbage Salad.
1 Cup Vinegar.
3 Tablespoons Sugar.
1 Cup Cream Or Milk.
1 Tablespoon Mustard.
3 Eggs, Beaten.
1 Tablespoon Butter Or 01!.
1 Tablespoon Salt.
 Mix, Boil And Cool, And Pour Over Cabbage.
Mrs. H. G. Ellis.

Italian Salad.

3 Medium Size Tomatoes.
2 Medium Size Onions.
1 Teaspoon Salt.
2 Sweet Mangoes.
4 Tablespoons Oil.
Dash Tobasco Sauce.
1 Tablespoon Sugar.
Vinegar.
Cut The Vegetables, And Add Dressing Made Of The Oil, Vinegar, Sugar And Salt.

Banana Salad.

Peel Bananas And Roll In Lemon Juice With Pinch Of Salt In It. Roll Bananas In Chopped Walnuts. Serve On Lettuce Leaf With Mayonnaise.

Salad Dressings.

No. 1.
1 Teaspoon Flour.
1 Small Teaspoon Salt.
2 Tablespoons Sugar.
2 Eggs, Well Beaten.
2 Tablespoons Butter.
3/4 Cup Cream.
1 Small Teaspoon Mustard.
3/4 Cup Vinegar.

Mrs. Newett.

No. 2
½ Pt. Cream.   1 Teaspoon Mustard.
½ Pt. Vinegar.   Butter Size Of Egg.
1 Cup Sugar.   Salt And Pepper.
3 Eggs Beaten.
Boil.   When Cold, Pour Over Cabbage.

Miss Jessie Macfarlane.

No. 3.

Yolks Of Two Eggs Ice Cold And Eight Tablespoons Olive Oil Ice Cold, Slowly Beaten Together. Add A Pinch Of Salt, One Teaspoon Made Mustard, Teaspoon Lemon Juice.

Miss Jessie Macfarlane.

No. 4.

1 Cup Mild Vinegar.   1 /2 Salt Spoon Cayenne Pepper.

Yolk Of 1 Egg.

½ Salt Spoon Turmeric Powder.

¾ Cup Sugar.

1 Desert Spoon Cornstarch.

1 Teaspoon Mustard.   1 Desert Spoon Butter.

Mix And Boil. Cool Before Using.

Mrs. L. C. Diggory.

Cold Dressing For Cabbage.

No. 1.

Yolks Of 2 Eggs Beaten Light.

Piece Of Butter Size Of Egg,
  Beat Again.

½ Cup Sugar.
  Beat Again.

½ Cup Mild Vinegar.

Pinch Of Salt.

Heat In Double Boiler. When Thick, Add One-Half Cup Cream, Stirring Constantly. When Cool Mix With Finely Cut Cabbage.

Mrs. W. L. Dean.

No. 2.

3 Eggs Beaten To Froth.

1 Teaspoon Black Pepper.

½ Cup Vinegar.

½ Cup Melted Butter,

1 Tablespoon Mixed Mustard.

Cook Eggs And Vinegar Together, Stirring Constantly Until It Thickens. Cool. Add The Other Ingredients. Sour Cream May Be Used Instead Of Butter.

Mrs. Franck.

No. 3.
3 Eggs.
3 Tablespoons Melted Butter.
1 Teaspoon Salt.
Dash Paprica.
6 Tablespoons Milk.
A Little Mustard.
1 Or 2 Tablespoons Vinegar.
   Beat Salt, Pepper And Eggs. Adci Other Ingredients. Put In Double Boiler And Stir Constantly Until Thick. When, Cool, Oil May Be Added.

Mrs. A. D. W. Smith.

No. 4.
Yolks Of 4 Eggs.
1 Teaspoon Salt.
4 Tablespoons Butter.
1/4 Teaspoon Pepper.
2 Tablespoons White Wine
1 Cup Cream.
Vinegar.

Mrs. M. D. Rosser.

No. 5
3 Tablespoons Of Vinegar.
Small Pinch Of Red Pepper.
1 Cup Of Water.
 1/2 Teaspoon Salt.
1 Teaspoon Sugar.
2 Eggs.
Butter Size Of Egg.
1 Teaspoon Of Sugar.

L Even Teaspoon Mustard.

3 Teaspoons Of Flour.

Boil The Vinegar And Water. Add Butter. Mix Other Ingredients. Pour The Vinegar And Water Over Them. If Not Stiff Enough, Cook A Few Minutes, Stirring Constantly. Nice For Either Cabbage Or Potatoes.

Mrs. Frederic Corss.

No. 6.

2 Eggs.

1 Teaspoon Mustard.

Butter Size Of Hickory Nut.

Salt And Pepper.

2 Tablespoons Sugar.

½ Cup Vinegar.

Boil All Together And Add Two-Thirds Cup Cream.

Mrs. C. W. Bixby.

No. 7.

1 Cup Cream, Scalded.   Mustard.

1 Egg.   1 Teaspoon Sugar.

Dash Of Cayenne.   1 Tablespoon Vinegar.

Salt.

Mix Egg And Seasoning Together And Add To Scalded Cream.   Do Not Boil Or It Will Curdle.

Mrs. Walter.

No. 8.

Juice Of One-Half Lemon Strained Into As Much Olive Oil. Shake In Fruit Jar Until Well Mixed. One-Half Cup Sour Cream, Two Teaspoons Sugar, ¼ Teaspoon Salt. Mix These And Pour Into Oil And Lemon Juice. Shake Until Well Blended.

Mrs. James S. Croll.

No. 9.

Yolks Of 4 Eggs.   8 Tablespoons Oil.

4 Tablespoons Vinegar.   1 Teaspoon Salt.
4 Teaspoons Sugar.   1 Dessertspoon Mustard.
1 Cup Whipped Cream, Or Whites Of 2 Eggs Beaten
Stiff.

Add Half The Oil To The Yolks, Then Slowly Add
Vinegar Cook In Double Boiler Until Thick, Stirring
Constantly. When Cold, Add Other Ingredients.

Mrs. Geo. F. Lee.

Pies

Mince Meat.

4 Lbs. Lean Meat.	9 Lbs. Apples.
1 1/2 Lbs. Suet.	3 Lbs. Raisins
2 Lbs. Currants.	1/2 Lb. Citron.
5 Lbs. Sugar.	3 Teaspoons Cloves.
10 Teaspoons Cinnamon.	5 Teaspoons Mace.
1 Teaspoon Black Pepper.	6tablespoons Salt.
1 Qt. Boiled Cider.	1 Pt. Molasses.

Juice And Rind Of Two Lemons And Three
Oranges. Sherry And Brandy To Taste. Keep In
Stone Jars. When Making Pies, Add More Liquor If
Necessary.

Miss Frances Dorrance.

Mince Meat.

2 Lbs. Suet.	3 Lbs. Raisins.
3 Lbs. Currants.	12 Lbs. Apples.
2 Lbs. Citron.	1 Oz. Cinnamon.
5 Lbs. Sugar.	1/2 Oz. Cloves.

1 Oz. Nutmeg.
1/2 Doz. Oranges And Lemons Chopped Fine.
¼ Oz. Mace.
2 Lbs. Meat, Tongue Preferred.
1 Pt. Wine.

Any Fruit Syrups May Be Used, Also Dates And
Figs.

Mrs. Snow.

Maple Syrup Pie.

Yolks 3 Eggs.   1 1/2 Tablespoons
Cornstarch.
1 ½ Cups Syrup.   Butter Size Of Walnut.
   Save Whites For Meringue.

Cream Pie.

1 Cup Cream.   2/3 Cup Sugar.
3 Eggs   1 Cup Raisins, Seeded And
Chopped.
   Reserve Whites For Meringue.
                                S. S. Goodwin.

Mince Meat.

4 Lbs. Lean Beef.   3 Lbs. Suet.
8 Lbs Apples.   3 Lbs. Currants.
3 Lbs. Raisins.   6 Lbs. Sugar.
2 Lbs. Citron.   Grated Rind 1 Orange.
1/2 Oz. Cinnamon.   1/4 Oz. Cloves.
¼ Oz. Mace.   4 Nutmegs.
3 Pts. Sweet Boiled Cider Or 1 Qt. Madeira Wine.
   This Makes About Three Gallons Mince Meat.
                        Miss Elizabeth Loveland.

Chocolate Pie.

1 Qt. Milk.   1 Square Chocolate.
Salt.   1 Cup Brown Sugar.
2 Eggs.   3 Tablespoons Cornstarch.
        Cook In Double Boiler.   Flavor With Vanilla. Bake
Crust First.
                        Mrs. Brewster.

Cocoanut Pie.

1 Cup Fresh Grated Cocoanut.   1 Cup Milk.
2 Tablespoons Flour.   1 Tablespoon Butter.
Yolks 2 Eggs.   Salt.
½ Cup Sugar.
   Put Cocoanut In Large Coffee Cup And Fill Up With

Milk. Mix Flour With Milk, And Boil Until Thick, Stir Constantly. Add Butter. When Cool, Beat In Yolks Of Eggs And Salt, Sugar And Cocoanut. Fill Crust. Reserve White For Meringue.

Mrs. E. G. Gage.

Mock Cherry Pie.

Cook Together Cranberries And Raisins. Sweeten As For Cranberry Jelly, Two Cups Sugar To One Quart Berries. Rake In A Two Crust Pie.

Mrs. E. E. Buckman.

Squash Pie.

1 Cup Hubbard Squash.	2 Cups Milk.
1 Teaspoon Cinnamon.	½ Teaspoon Ginger.
Yolks 2 Eggs.	3 Tablespoons Sugar.

Steam And Strain Squash. Salt. Bring To Boil Squash And Milk And Spices. Beat Eggs And Sugar; Add The Milk And Squash And Thoroughly Mix. Flavor With Vanilla. Cool Before Baking In A Paste-Lined Pie Tin.

Mrs. E. E. Buckman.

Raisin Pie.

1 Lemon.	1 Cup Raisins.
1 Cup Water.	1 Cup Cracker Crumbs.

Boil Lemon, Raisins And Water, Add Cracker Crumbs.

Mrs. Wesley Hilbert.

Lemon Pie.

2 Lemons.	12 Or 14 Crackers.
1 Qt. Water.	2 Or 3 Eggs.

Grate Lemons, Roll Crackers, Pour On Boiling Water And Let Cool. Beat In Eggs. This Makes Three Pies.

Mrs. Wesley Hilbert.

Pumpkin Pie.

1 Qt. Stewed Pumpkin.	1 Qt. Milk.
4 Eggs.	1 Cup Sugar.

Pinch Salt.   1 Teaspoon Nger.
Stew And Rub Pumpkin Through Colander Before
Measuring.

> Miss Frances Dorrance.

Pumpkin Pie.
Small Pumpkin, Boiled, Drained And Put Through
Colander.
Milk To Thin.
Sweeten.
Flavor With   Nutmeg And Cinnamon.
Whites 3 Eggs Beaten Stiff.
Butter Size Of An Egg.

> Mrs. Gregory.

Lemon Pie.
1 Cup Sugar.   1 Tablespoon Butter.
3 Eggs.   2 Tablespoons Cornstarch.
1 Cup Boiling Water. 1 Grated Lemon.
   Boil Until Clear. Bake Crust, Then Pour In Custard And
Make Meringue Of Whites Of Eggs.

> Mrs. J. D. Flanagan.

Rhubarb Pie.
1 ½ Cups Rhubarb, Chopped Fine.
1 Level Tablespoon Flour.
1 Egg.
1 Cup Sugar.
Small Piece Of Butter.
   Bake In Two Crusts.

> Mrs. J. D. Flanagan.

Potato Pie.
1 Pt. Cream.   4 Eggs.
1 Lb. Sugar.   1 Lemon, Juice And Rind.
1 Lb. Mashed Potatoes.
   Rub Cream, Sugar And Potatoes Through Seive Bake
Like Custard Pie.

> Miss Frances Dorrance.

Lemon Pie.

Yolks Of 4 Eggs.

1 Lemon, Grated.

1 Tablespoon Sugar.

1 Tablespoon Cornstarch

1 Tablespoon Butter

1 Tablespoon Milk.

Reserve Whites For Meringue.

Mrs. D. H. Eavenson.

Orange Pie.

Yolks 2 Eggs.

Cornstarch

1 Heaping Tablespoon Flour.

Salt.

1 Even Tablespoon

1 Pt. Milk.

½ Cup Sugar.

Beat Eggs And Sugar, Add Flour, Dissolve Cornstarch And Salt In A Little Cold Milk, Pour Into Boiling Milk And Cook About Three Minutes. Cool And Flavor With Extract Of Orange. Pour In Baked Crust. Make Meringue Of Whites Of Eggs And One-Half Cup Sugar; Flavor With Orange Extract.

Mrs. John Nugent.

Lemon Raisin Pie.

1 ¼ Cups Cold Water.

1 Egg.

1 Cup Chopped Raisins.

Lemon.

½ Cup Sugar.

1 Teaspoon Cornstarch.

Grated Rind Of One

Squeeze Juice Into Water, Sugar, Etc.

Miss Raub.

Lemon Pie.

1 Cup Sugar.

1 Cup Hot Water.

Small Piece Butter.

1 Tablespoon Cornstarch.

2 Eggs.

Juice And Rind Of Lemon

Use Whites Of Eggs For Meringue.

Miss Jessie Macfarlane.

Lemon Cream Pie.

½ Cup Sugar.

Piece Butter Size Of Egg.

Yolks Of 2 Eggs.

White Of 1 Egg.

1 Pt. Milk.   Juice And Rind Of Lemon.
2 Heaping Tablespoons Cornstarch.
    Bake Crust. Wet The Cornstarch With A Little Milk.
Cook All The Ingredients Together In Double Boiler Until
Thick And Smooth. Stir Constantly. Make Meringue Of
Other White And One Tablespoon Powdered Sugar.

                                Mrs. T. W. Thomas.

Pie Crust.

4 Tablespoons Lard.   1 Cup Flour.
4 Tablespoons Cold Water.   1 Pinch Salt.
    Rub Thoroughly Together; Roll Out Without Kneading.

                                Mrs. C. Bach.

Rhubarb Pie.

1 ½ Cups Sugar.   1 Egg.
2 Teacups Raw Rhubarb.   ½ Cup Chopped Raisins.
Pinch Of Salt.   Lump Of Butter.
    Bake In Two Crusts. Cut Rhubarb, Add One-Fourth
Teaspoon Soda, Cover With Boiling Water And Let Stand
Until Cool.   Drain And Add Other Ingredients.

Puddings

English Plum Pudding.

1 Lb. Flour.   1 Qt. Sweet Milk.
1 Lb. Grated Bread.   6 Eggs.
1 Lb. Beef Suet Chopped Fine.   1 Nutmeg.
1 Lb. Brown Sugar.   1 Teaspoon Allspice.
1 Lb. Raisins.   ½ Teaspoon Cinnamon.
1 Lb. Currants.   1/2 Teaspoon Cloves.
¼ Lb. Citron.   1 Glass Brandy.
    Beer May Be Used Instead Of Milk And Brandy. Boil
Five Hours Without Stopping, In Well Floured Bag. When
Served, Pour Brandy Over And Light. Serve With Hot
Brandy Sauce.

                                Miss Elizabeth Loveland.

84

English Plum Pudding.

2 Lbs. Raisins.	1 Pt. Bread Crumbs.
1 Lb. Currants.	1 Cup Molasses.
1 Lb. Brown Sugar.	1 Teaspoon Cinnamon.
1 Lb. Chopped Suet.	4 Eggs.
1 Lb. Flour.	Nutmeg.
¼ Lb. Citron.	½ Teaspoon Cloves.
¼ Lb. Almonds.	½ Teaspoon Soda.

Steam Six Hours.

Mrs. Pierce Butler.

Suet Pudding.

1 Cup Flour.	1/2 Cup Raisins.
1/2 Cup Suet.	1 Egg.
½ Cup Milk.	1 Teaspoon Soda.
½ Cup Molasses.	Salt And Spices To Taste.

Steam Twenty Minutes In Egg Poacher.

Mrs. R. B. Vaughn.

Plain Plum Pudding.

1 Cup Sweet Milk.	1 Teaspoon Soda.
1 Cup N. O. Molasses.	1 Teaspoon Cinnamon And

Nutmeg.

1 ½ Cups Suet Chopped Fine.

Flour Enough To Make Spoon Stand Upright.

2 Cups Raisins.	Pinch Of Salt.
2 Cups Currants.	3 Eggs.

Steam Four Hours.

Miss Jessie Macfarlane.

Plum Pudding.

1 ½ Cups Chopped Suet.	2 Cups Currants.
1 Cup Milk.	1 Cup Citron.
1 Cup Molasses.	½ Teaspoon Soda.
2 Cups Dried Bread Crumbs.	1 Teaspoon Cloves.
1 Cup Flour.	½ Teaspoon Salt.
2 Cups Raisins.	1 Nutmeg.

Steam Four Hours.

Mrs. R. A. Hutchison.

Poor Man's Pudding

1 Cup Chopped Suet Or Butter. 1 Heaping Teaspoon Of Baking Powder.

1 Cup Molasses. 2 Teaspoons Cinnamon.

2 Cups Sweet Milk. 1/2 Teaspoon Cloves.

2 Eggs. ½ Nutmeg Grated.

1 Qt. Flour. 1 Large Cup Of Raisins.

1 Even Teaspoon Of Soda.

Currants And Citron May Be Added. If Made With Suet Add ½ Teaspoon Of Salt; If With Butter, Add A Very Little Salt. Steam Three Hours.

Mrs. Von Krug.

Plum Pudding.

1 Cup Bread Crumbs. ½ Cup Currants.

1 Cup Flour. 2 Eggs Well Beaten.

1 Cup Sugar. ½ Teaspoon Soda.

1 Cup Chopped Suet Or Butter.

2 Teaspoons Cinnamon.

I Cup Sweet Milk. 1 1/2 Teaspoons Cloves.

1 Cup Raisins. ½ Teaspoon Salt.

Steam Three Hours.

Mrs. J. R. Davis.

Harford Pudding.

1 Cup Suet Chopped Fine.

1 Cup Flour.

1 Cup Sour Milk.

½ Teaspoon Soda.

1 Cup Molasses.

Salt.

1 Cups Raisins.

Steam Three Hours.

Mrs. T. L. Welles.

Hard Times Pudding.

1 Cup Molasses. 1 Teaspoon Of Cloves.

1 Cup Buttermilk.

1 Cup Suet Chopped Fine. Dissolved In Warm Water.

1 Cup Raisins. Batter.

1 Cup Currants.

1 Teaspoon Cinnamon.

½ Teaspoon Salt.

1 Teaspoon Of Soda

Flour Enough For Thick

Boil In Buttered Mould Three Hours.

Miss Elizabeth Loveland.

Ashburton Pudding.

1 Cup Molasses.

4 Cups Flour.

1 Cup Butter. Sliced.

1 Cup Sour Milk.

4 Eggs.

1 Teaspoon Of Soda.

1 ½ Cream Nuts Blanched And

1 Or 2 Cups Raisins.

Boil Or Steam Three Hours.

Mrs. George Shoemaker.

Indian Pudding.

1 Qt. Milk Scalded

1 egg

1 cup molasses

1/2 Teaspoon Ginger.

7 Even Tablespoons Yellow Corn Meal.

Pinch Of Salt.

Mix Molasses, Meal, Egg, Salt And Ginger Together And Stir Into Scalding Milk Until Slightly Thickened. Bake In Pudding Dish Two And One-Half Hours. Bake Slowly Or Pudding Will Burn. Serve Hot With Butter.

Mrs. F. L. Olds.

Graham Pudding.

1 Cup Sweet Milk.

1 Cup Molasses.

2 Cups Graham Flour.

1 Teaspoon Soda.

2 Cups Seeded Raisins.

Salt.

Spices.

Steam Two And One-Half Hours.

Dark Steamed Pudding.
1 Cup Brown Sugar Or
Molasses.
1 1/2 Cups Raisins.
1 Cup Sweet milk.
3 Cups Flour.
1 Teaspoon Baking Powder.
1 Cup Suet Chopped Fine.
        Steam Two To Three Hours.
                        Mrs. Brewster

Whole Wheat Pudding.
2 Cups Whole Wheat Flour.   1 Egg Well Beaten.
1 Cup Sweet Milk.   1 Even Teaspoon Soda.
1 Cup Molasses.   Salt.
1 Cup Chopped Raisins.   Spices To Taste.
   Steam Three Hours.

                        Miss Helen Goodwin.

Marmalade Pudding.
1 Cup Suet.
3 Eggs, Whites And Yolks Beaten Separately
1 Cup Sugar.
½ Cup Flour.
1 ½ Cups Bread Crumbs.
Season To Taste.
1 Teaspoon Salt.
2 Tablespoons Marmalade.
   Steam Two Hours.
                        Mrs. William Callam.

Fresh Plum Pudding.
1 Cup Chopped Suet.   1 Teaspoon Baking Powder.
2 Cups Flour (Large.) Milk Enough To Make
Thick Batter.
1 Teaspoon Salt.

Stir Full Of Fresh Plums, Cut In Half, Or Sour Cherries Or Huckleberries. Boil In Buttered Mould Three Hours. Eat With Hot Sauce.

Miss Elizabeth Loveland.

Honey-Comb Pudding.

1 Pt. Molasses.
1 Cup Brown Sugar.
Butter Size Of Egg.
1 Cup Milk.

1 Teaspoon Soda,
6 Eggs.
1 Cup Flour,
Mace And Cloves.

Beat Molasses And Sugar Together. Melt Butter And Soda In Milk, And Pour Into Molasses. Add Yolks Of Eggs, Stir In Dour, Mace, Cloves And Whites Of Eggs Beaten Stiff. Bake One Hour In Moderate Oven.

Mrs. W. F. Church.

Brown Pudding.

¼ Cup Butter.
Cloves.
½ Cup Molasses.
1 Cup Sweet Milk.
2 Eggs.
Soda.
2 Cups Whole Wheat Flour.
1 Heaping Teaspoon Baking Powder.
1 Heaped Teaspoon Cinnamon.

1/8 Teaspoon

¼ Teaspoon Salt.
Dash Of Nutmeg.
1small Half Teaspoon

Steam Two And One-Half Hours. Eat With Hard Or Creamy Sauce.

Mrs. Von Krug

Huckelberry Pudding.

1 Cup Molasses.
1 Cup Berries.
½ Cup Warm Water.
Butter Size Of Egg.
Boil Two Hours.

1 Teaspoon Soda.
1 Teaspoon Cloves.
1 Teaspoon Cinnamon.
2 Cups Flour.

Mrs. C. W. Bixby.

Huckelberry Pudding.

2 Tablespoons Butter.

1 Cup Brown Sugar.

2 Eggs.

½ Teaspoon Cinnamon.

1/2 Teaspoon Cloves.

A Little Nutmeg

½ Cup Flour.

1 Pt. Berries.

½ Teaspoon Soda.

Mrs. Meginess.

Huckelberry Pudding.

1 Good Pint Sifted Flour.

½ Teaspoon Salt.

2 Teaspoons Baking Powder.

½ Cup Sugar.

1 Cup Sweet Milk.

1 Egg.

¼ Cup Butter.

1 Heaping Cup Huckleberries (Sprinkled With Flour And Stirred In Last).

Serve Warm With Cream.

Mrs. W. L. Dean.

Orange Souffle.

½ Box Gelatine.

Juice Of Five Oranges (One Pint).

1 Pt. Whipped Cream.

Bit Of Orange Rind.

1/2 Cup Cold Water.

1/4 Cup Hot Water.

2/3 Cup Sugar.

Soak Gelatine In Cold Water Thirty Minutes. Add Hot Water And When Dissolved Add Sugar, Orange Juice, And Orange Rind. Strain And When It Begins To Thicken Stir In Whipped Cream. Put In Mould On Ice. Serve With Whipped Cream.

Miss Nellie Parry.

Corn Pudding.

1 Pt. Milk With

1 Tablespoon Flour.

1 Tablespoon Butter.

1 Tablespoon Sugar

4 Eggs.

Salt.

Add To Corn Grated From Six Large Ears.

Mrs. Gregory.

Lemon Pudding.

1 Pt. Bread Crumbs.

Yolks Of Three Eggs.

1 Qt. Milk.   Sweeten To Taste.
Juice And Grated Rind Of One Lemon.
   Bake Twenty Or Twenty-Five Minutes. When
Baked Cover With Meringue Made From The Beaten
Whites.

Mrs. E. G. Gage.

Cheese Pudding.

   In Buttered Dish Place Alternate Layers Of
Broken Cracker, Cheese, Salt, Pepper And Butter.
Pour Milk Over All And Bake.

Mrs. R. B. Vaughn.

Carrot Pudding.

¼ Lb. Grated Carrot.	1 Egg.
¼ Lb. Chopped Suet.	¼ Lb. Brown Sugar.
½ Lb. Flour.	Spices To Taste.
¼ Lb. Raisins.	Salt.
¼ Lb. Currants.	

   Steam Two Hours.

Miss Nellie Parry.

Cottage Pudding.

¼ Cup Butter.	1 Egg.
1 Cup Sugar.	1 Teaspoon Baking Powder.
1 Cup Milk.	Pinch Of Salt.
2 Cups Flour.	

Mix As For Cake And Bake In Quick Oven.

Miss Elizabeth Loveland.

Tapioca Cream.

2 Tablespoons Tapioca.	4 Eggs.
1 Qt. Milk.	Little Sugar.

   Soak The Tapioca Two Hours. Cook Half An Hour
In The Boiling Milk. Beat The Yolks Of The Eggs
With The Sugar, Add Them To The Tapioca And
Cook Three Minutes. Take From Fire And Stir In
Whites Of Eggs Beaten Stiff. Serve Cold.

Miss Esther French.

Sunderland Pudding.

1 Pt. Milk.   3 Tablespoons Flour.
6 Eggs.   A Little Salt.

Beat The Eggs Separately. Rub The Flour Smooth In A Little Milk. Beat The Eggs Into The Flour And Milk, Yolks First Then Whites. Add The Rest Of The Milk. Bake In Quick Oven. Serve Hot With Hot Sauce.

Mrs. George Shoemaker.

Chocolate Blanc Mange.

Cover 1 Oz. Gelatine With Water. Boil 1 Pt. Milk Five Minutes With 4 Oz. Chocolate And 12 Oz. Sugar.

Add Gelatine And Boil Five Minutes Longer, Stirring Constantly. Flavor With Vanilla And Pour Into Moulds To Cool. Serve With Cream Or A Rich Custard Sauce.

Miss Esther French.

American Cream.

½ Cup Cold Water.   2 Eggs.
¼ Cup Gelatine.   1/2 Cup Sugar.
1 Pt. Milk.   1 Teaspoon Vanilla.

Let The Milk Come To Boil. Add The Yolks Of Eggs Beaten With Sugar.   Stir In Whites Of Eggs When Cold.

Mrs. D. H. Eavenson.

Aunt Peggy's Apple Dumplings.

1 Pt. Flour.   Salt.
1 Teaspoon Baking Powder.   Butter Or Lard Size Of Egg.

Mix With Milk Or Water Into Rather Soft Dough. Roll Out And Divide Dough Into Five Or Six Strips Three Inches Wide.   Spread Apples Cut Into Thin Slices On Strips And Roll Up Like Cinnamon Buns. Put Close Together In Deep Bread Pan And Pour

Over Them. 34 Cup Sugar. 1 Tablespoon Butter.
Pinch Of Cinnamon. Hot Milk Enough To Fill The
Cup.
Bake Thirty Minutes.   Serve With Cream Or Sauce.
Mrs. B. R. Tubbs.

Cottage Pudding.

1 Cup Flour.	2 Eggs.
1 Cup Sugar.	2 Teaspoons Baking Powder.
½ Cup Milk.	Butter Size Of Egg.

Miss Raub.

Vanilla Souffle.

1 Cup Milk.	¼ Teaspoon Salt.
2 Tablespoons Flour.	1 Teaspoon Vanilla.
3 Tablespoons Sugar.	4 Eggs.
2 Tablespoons Butter.	

Scald Milk With Salt In Double Boiler. Add Butter
And Flour Rubbed Together. Cook Ten Minutes
Stirring Constantly. Turn Into Yolks Of Eggs Which
Have Been Beaten To Cream With Sugar. When Cool
Fold In Lightly The Beaten Whites Of The Eggs,
And Bake In Buttered Pudding Dish In Moderate
Oven Thirty Or Forty Minutes. Serve At Once With
Sauce.

Miss Esther French.

Frozen Mocha Tart

3 Eggs.	5c. Worth Candied Cherries, Chopped.
1 Pt. Cream—Whipped.	5c. Worth Pineapple, Chopped.
1 Cup Sugar.	5c. Worth English Walnuts, Chopped.
8 Almond Macaroons.	2 Tablespoons Mocha.

Heat Whites Of Eggs, Add Sugar, Then Yolks, Cream,
Fruits, And Macaroons Rolled Fine. Flavor With Mocha
And Put In Mould.

Steam Batter Pudding.

1 Pt. Milk.   1 Cup Flour.
4 Eggs.   ½ Teaspoon Salt.

Beat Eggs Light, Add Milk. Pour Into Flour And Beat Until Smooth. Steam One And One-Quarter Hours In Buttered Mould. Serve With Hard Sauce Or Cream And Sugar.

Mrs. B. R. Tubbs.

Peach Pudding.

1 Cup Sugar.   1 Egg.
1/2 Cup Sweet Milk.   1 Tablespoon
Butter.
1 ½ Teaspoons Baking Powder.   1 ½ Cups Flour.
Salt.

Fill Baking Dish One-Third Full Of Sliced Peaches, Well Sugared. Over This Pour The Batter. Bake One Hour Serve With Cream Or Hard Sauce.

Mrs. B. R. Tubbs.

Orange Blanc Mange.

½ Cup Sugar.   1 Box Gelatine.
2 Cups Boiling Water.   4 Tablespoons Orange
Juice.
1 Tablespoon Lemon Juice.   Whites 3 Eggs.
Salt.   Wine.

Mrs. B. R. Tubbs.

Chocolate Pudding.

1 Qt. Bread Crumbs.   Vanilla.
8 Tablespoons Grated Chocolate.   1 Qt. Milk.
6 Tablespoons Sugar.   Salt.
Butter Size Of Egg.

Soak Bread Crumbs In Hot Milk And Add Other Ingredients. Bake One And A Half Hours In Moderate Oven. Serve Hot.

Mrs. H. C. Miller.

Lemon Creams.

1 Lemon, Grated.   Yolks 4 Eggs.

4 Tablespoons Sugar.   4 Tablespoons Cold Water.

   Beat Eggs, Sugar And Water. Let Simmer, Stirring Constantly Until Thick. Add Beaten Whites. Serve In Glasses With Crackers.

                                        Mrs. B. R. Tubbs

Snow Balls.

½ Cup Butter.   ½ Cup Sugar.

1 Cup Flour.   ½ Cup Corn Starch.

3 Teaspoons Baking Powder. ½ Cup Milk.

Whites 4 Eggs.

   Cream Butter And Sugar. Sift Flour, Cornstarch And Baking Powder. To This Add Milk And Stir In Gently Whites Beaten Stiff. Steam In Buttered Cups For One-Half Hour. Turn Out And Roll In Powdered Sugar. Serve With Fruit Sauce.   Makes Six.

                                        Mrs. D. M. Rosser.

Chocolate Sponge.

4 Eggs.   1 ½ Oz. Chocolate Melted.

½ Lb. Granulated Sugar.   1 Large Teaspoon Vanilla.

1/6 Box Gelatine.

   Soak Gelatine In Small Cup Warm Water One-Half Hour. Beat Yolks Of Eggs And Sugar Together Until Very Light, Add Chocolate And Mix With Gelatine. Beat The Whites Very Stiff, Add Vanilla And Stir Lightly Into Chocolate Mixture Until All Is Stiff. Pour Into Punch Glasses And Serve With Whipped Cream.

                                        Mrs. H. B. Payne.

Crumb Pudding.

2 Cups Bread Or Cracker Crumbs Rolled Fine.

1 Cup Raisins.   2/3 Cup Sugar.

1 Cup Flour.   1 Teaspoon Soda.

1 Cup Suet Or Butter.   Spices And Salt To Taste.

1 ½ Cups Buttermilk Or Sour Milk.

Boil Or Steam One Hour.

Mrs. C. Bach.

Apple Dumplings.
1 Pt. Sifted Flour.
1 Teaspoon Baking Powder Sifted With Flour.
Butter Size Of Walnut.
Salt.
Milk To Make Soft Dough.
  Have Boiling In Deep Baking Pan,—
1 Pt. Water.
34 Cup Sugar.
Butter Size Of Egg.
  Put Dumplings In Pan And Bake.

Raisin Puffs.
2 Eggs.   2 Cups Flour.
1 ½ Cup Of Milk.   2 Teaspoons Of Sugar.
3 Level Teaspoons Of Baking Powder.
1 Cup Of Raisins, Chopped Very Fine And Dredged
In Flour.
Steam Forty-Five Minutes In Small Cups.

Mrs. William Callam.

Pudding Sauces

Chocolate Sauce.
2 Cups Sugar.   ¾ Cup Chocolate.
1 Cup Cream.   1 Teaspoon Vanilla.
Boil Sugar, Cream And Chocolate Together Five
Minutes, Stirring Constantly. Add Vanilla. Serve
Hot.

Mrs. Andrew Raub.

Sauce For Cottage Pudding.
1 Cup Powdered Sugar.
2½ Cup Butter.

3 Eggs (Yolks).
Beat Half An Hour. Flavor With Wine. Improved By Adding A Little Cream.

Miss Raub.

Sauce For Whole Wheat Pudding.
1 Cup Sugar.　　　　　　1 Egg, Well Beaten.
1 Heaping Tablespoon Flour.　1 Pt. Water.
½ Cup Butter.
Sift Flour Into Sugar. Rub In Butter. Add Egg And Water. Flavor To Taste.

Miss Helen Goodwin.

Vanilla Dip.
1 Cup Sugar (Small.)
Piece Butter.
1 Tablespoon Flour.
Mix And Pour On Boiling Water. Boil Ike Gravy. Flavor With Vanilla.

Mrs. Meginess.

Hard Sauce.
2 Cups Sugar.
½ Cup Butter.
Cream Together Half An Hour And Add The Unbeaten Whites Of Two Eggs. Flavor To Taste.

Mrs. J. R. Davis.

Strawberry Sauce.
2 Tablespoons Butter.
1 Cup Powdered Sugar.
Yolk Of 1 Egg.
Cream Butter. Beat In One-Half Cup Fruit Or Jam. Chill Before Using.

Mrs. D. M. Rosser.

Sauce.
1 Cup Sugar.　　　　　　1 Egg.

½ Cup Butter.   Lemon Or 4 Tablespoons
Sherry.
½ Cup Boiling Water.
  Beat Butter And Sugar Very Light, Stir In Yolk Of
Egg Well Beaten, Then Lemon Juice And Grated
Rind, And Steam In Double Boiler, Stirring
Constantly, Till It Smokes, Not Boils. When Hot,
Add White Of Egg Well Beaten And One-Half Cup
Hot Water.   Serve At Once
                              Mrs. Geo. Shoemaker.

Cream Sauce.
2 Eggs.   4 Tablespoons
Sugar.
2/3 Cup Whipped Cream.   Wine To
Taste.
  Whip Whites And Yolks Of Eggs Very Stiff. Whip
In Cream, Sugar And Wine.
                              Mrs. C. W. Bixby.

Hard Sauce.
¼ Cup Butter.
1 Tablespoon Brandy Or Vanilla
I Cup Powdered Sugar.
Whites Of Two Eggs.
  Cream Butter And Sugar, Add Eggs Gradually
And Beat Until Very Light. Sprinkle With Nutmeg.
                              Mrs. R. B. Vaughn.

Chocolate Sauce.
I Square Melted Chocolate.   ½ Cup Sugar,
1 Cup Milk.   1 Teaspoon Vanilla.
  Cook Chocolate And Milk Until Smooth. Add
Sugar And Vanilla.
                              M. A. Van Scoy.

Foaming Sauce.
2 Cups Sugar.

1 Egg.

I Cup Butter.

  1 Teaspoon Corn Starch Dissolved In Little Cold Water. Slowly Fill Cup In Which Corn Starch Is Dissolved With Boiling Water. Pour Into Other Ingredients Which Have Been Beaten To A Cream And Cook A Few Minutes. Flavor.

Mrs. W. L. Dean.

Sauce For Crumb Pudding.

1 Cup Sugar.	Nutmeg.
½ Cup Butter.	Salt.
½ Cup Flour.	2 Cups Boiling

Water.

 Boil Five Minutes.

Sauce For Apple Pudding.

1 ½ Cups Water.	2 Tablespoons Cornstarch.
½ Cup Butter.	1 Tablespoon Vanilla.
5 Tablespoons Sugar.	

Frozen Desserts

Frozen Peaches.

2 Lbs. Very Ripe Peaches.

1 Qt. Water.

1 1/2 Lbs. Sugar.

  Boil Sugar And Water. When Cool Add Peaches Mashed Through Sieze. Freeze. This Is Enough For Eight Large Dishes.

Miss Elizabeth Loveland.

Peach Ice Cream.

1 Pt. Milk.	1 Lb. Sugar.
1 Pt. Cream.	6 Large, Ripe Peaches

  Scald Milk And Cream Together, Take From Fire And Dissolve One-Half The Sugar. Mash The

Peaches Through A Sieve And Add Reminder Of Sugar. Add Peaches To Milk When Cool And Freeze. Miss Elizabeth Loveland.

Ice Cream In Melons.
Pack Strawberry Ice Cream In Halved Gem Musk Melons And Garnish With Halved Berries.

Mrs. Geo. F. Lee.

Frozen Fruits.
2 Lbs. Sugar.
1 Qt. Peaches.
1 Qt. Pineapple.
1 Qt. Boiling Water.
1 Heaping Tablespoon Flour Mixed Smooth With Cold Water And Scalded With The Boiling Water. Grind The Fruit, Mix Ali Together And Freeze.

Mrs. D. H. Eavenson.

Sicilian Sherbet.
1 Can Peaches.   Whites Of
Two Eggs Beaten
1 Pt. Orange Juice. Light.   1 Pt. Sugar.
Press Peaches Through Colander, Add Orange Juice And Sugar And Stir Until Sugar Is Dissolved. Put In Freezer And When Partly Frozen Stir In Whites Of Eggs. Stir Beater A Few Times And Let Stand About An Hour.

White Velvet Sherbet.
Juice Of Three Lemons.   1 Qt. Milk.
1/4 Cups Sugar.   1 Teaspoon Lemon Extract.
Add Milk Slowly To Lemon Juice And Sugar. Freeze At Once.

Mrs. James H. Hughes.

Sherbet.
3 Pts. Water.   Juice Of 3 Lemons.

3 Cups Sugar.   3 Bananas Chopped Fine.
Juice Of 3 Oranges.   Whites Of 3 Eggs.
Boil Water And Sugar To A Syrup. When Cool Add
The Fruit. When Nearly Frozen Add The Beaten
Whites. Very Nice If Garnished With Cherries When
Served.

Mrs. James H. Hughes.

Sherbet.
To 2 Cups Sugar Boiled Five Minutes,
Add — 3 Qts. Water. 3 Grated Lemons. Juice Of
Four Oranges.
   Freeze And When Frozen Add Whites Of Three
Eggs Beaten.

Nellie Grover.

Maple Mousse.
1 Large Cup Maple Syrup.
Yolks Of Four Eggs, Beaten Light.
   Stir Together And Cook Slowly Until It Thickens.
Cool, Beat Well While Cooling And Add The
Mixture To I Pt. Cream Whipped Very Light. Beat
Well Together And Put In Freezer From Two To
Three Hours. Use More Salt Than When Churning
It.

Mrs. Andrew Raub.

Chocolate Sauce For Vanilla Ice Cream.
1 Pt. Milk.
2 Eggs.
1 Tablespoon Corn Starch.
1 Teaspoon Vanilla Or Sherry.
3 Oz. Bakers Chocolate. Ry.
1 Small Cup Powdered Sugar.
   Scrape Chocolate And Dissolve With Two
Tablespoons Of The Sugar And Two Tablespoons
Boiling Water. Mix Cornstarch With A Little Of The
Milk Then Put With Rest Of Milk And Dissolved
Chocolate In Double Boiler. Drop Yolks Of Eggs

Into This Custard. Beat Whites Of Eggs With Rest Of Sugar And Add The Last Thing To The Custard. Serve Boiling Hot.

Miss Frances Dorrance.

Cakes

Fruit Cake.

3 Cups Sugar.	2 Teaspoons Soda.
1 1/2 Cups Butter.	½ Lb. Currants.
6 Eggs.	3/ Lb. Raisins.
1 ½ Cups Sour Cream.	¼ Citron.
Flour.	1 Nutmeg.

   Add Sugar And Butter To Beaten Eggs. Dissolve Soda In Warm Water And Put Into Cake While Warm. Scald Raisins And Dredge With Flour. Put Citron Into Cake In Thin Slices As You Pour Cake Into Pans.   Make Cake Thick.

Phoebe Mott.

Black Fruit Cake.

1 Lb. Butter.	½ Pt. Brandy.
1 Lb. Sugar.	1 Gill Orange
Water.	
1 Lb. Flour.	2 Oranges, Rind
And Juice.	
2 4 Lbs. Raisins.	1 Teaspoon Vanilla.
1 ½ Lbs. Citron.	2 Large Nutmegs.
2 Lbs. Currants.	2 Even
Tablespoons Cloves.	
3 2 ½ Lbs. Dates.	1 Tablespoon
Ginger.	
1 Lb. Jordan Almonds.	4 Heaping
Tablespoons Cinnamon.	
10 Eggs.	1 Pt. Molasses.

Rub Sugar, Butter And Unbeaten Yolks To Cream. Add Unbeaten Whites And Beat Very Light. Put In Molasses Then Flour, Fruit And Spices—Brandy Last. Bake From Three To Four Hours In Slow Oven.
Miss Elizabeth Loveland.

Mother's Fruit Cake.

1 ½ Cups Butter.   ¼ Lb. Orange Pe
2 Cups Sugar.   1 Lb. Raisins.
7 Eggs.   1 Lb. Currants.
1 Cup Sweet Milk.   2 Cups Flour.
1/4lb. Citron.
2 Teaspoons Baking Powder.
¼ Lb. Lemon Peel.

Add Eggs One At A Time To Creamed Butter And Sugar. Cut Citron, Lemon And Orange Peel Fine. Bake Two And One-Half Hours In Moderate Oven.
Mrs. Albert R. Miller.

Bethlehem Black Cake.

3 Cups Sugar.   1 Tablespoon Soda.
½ Cup Butter.   1 Tablespoon Cinnamon.
1 Cup Sour Milk.   ½ Tablespoon Cloves.
3 Eggs.   Raisins, Citron, Currants.
3 Cups Flour.

Miss Esther French.

Farmers' Fruit Cake.

3 Cups Dried Apples.   1 Cup Sweet Milk.
2 Cups Molasses.   1 Cup Chopped Raisins.
¾ Cup Butter.   1 ½ Teaspoons Soda.
1 Cup Sugar.   Spices To Taste.
Flour To Make Stiff Batter.

Soak Apples In Warm Water Over Night. Chop Slightly In Morning And Simmer Two Hours In Molasses. Add Other Ingredients And Bake In Quick Oven.
Mrs. Brewster.

Dutch Bread.

1 Pt. Milk Scalded.	1 Cup Currants.
½ Cup Butter.	2 Eggs.
1 Cup Sugar.	Flour For Stiff Batter.

Beat Very Thoroughly. When Cold Add Little Yeast And Let Stand Over Night. In The Morning Spread Out In Pan And Cover Top With Bits Of Sugar, Bmter And Cinnamon. Mrs. C. W. Bixby.

Dutch Cake.

1 Cup Sugar.	½ Cup Sweet Milk.
1 1/2 Cups Flour.	2 Teaspoons Baking Powder.
½ Cup Butter.	2 Eggs.

Mix Sugar, Flour, Butter And Baking Powder Into Crumbs. Take Out One-Half Cup Of Crumbs And To The Remainder Add Eggs, Well Beaten, And Milk Gradually. Turn Into Pan And Cover With The Half Cup Of Crumbs Which Has Been Reserved.

Mrs. Keller.

Dutch Cake.

Mix Well Together:

1 Cup Sugar.

1 Cup Yeast.

1 Cup Mashed Potatoes.

Let Rise Four Hours And Add:

2 Eggs.

½ Cup Butter.

Salt.

Flour Enough To Mould Into Loaf.

Let It Rise Over Night. In The Morning Put In Pie Pans To Rise Until Light. Bake Ten Minutes. Brush Over With Melted Butter, Sprinkle With Sugar And Cinnamon And Return To Oven A Few Minutes To Harden.   Makes Four Cakes

Mrs. Benner

Dutch Cake.

2 Eggs, Yolks And Whites Beaten Separately.

| 2 ½ Cups Flour. | 2 Tablespoons Baking |

Powder.

1 Cup Sugar.　　　　　　　1 Cup Of Milk.

Mix Butter, Sugar And Yolks Of Eggs Together; Add Milk, Flour And Baking Powder. Fold In Whites, Sprinkle With Cinnamon And Sugar And Bake In Moderate Oven.

Mrs. A. D. W. Smith.

Dutch Cake.

1 Tablespoon Butter Mixed With 1 Cup Milk
1 Cup Flour, And 1 Cup Sugar.
Then Add: 1 Cup Flour Mixed With 1 Egg And 2 Teaspoons Baking Powder.
　Put In Long Pan And Cover With Cinnamon And Sugar.

Mrs. James S. Croll.

Dutch Apple Cake.

2 Cups Flour.　　　　　　　1 Cup Milk.
½ Teaspoon Baking Powder.　3 Tablespoons Sugar.
2 Tablespoons Butter.　　　　4 Or 5 Large Sour Apples.
　Mix Thoroughly And Bake One-Half Hour,

Mrs. Hilbert.

Dutch Cake.

1 Tablespoon Butter Mixed With 1 Cup Flour.
Then Add: ½ Cup Sugar.
1 Cup Milk Or Water.
1 Egg.
Mix Well And Add:
1 Cup Flour.
2 Tablespoons Baking Powder.
　Sprinkle Generously With Sugar And Cinnamon.

Dutch Cake.

　Stir Together.
　1 Cup Sugar.
Piece Of Butter Size Of Egg
1 Cup Flour.
　Work Butter In With Hands.
　Then Add:

1 Egg Beaten Light. 1 Cup Milk.

Then Add :

1 Cup Flour Mixed With 2 Teaspoons Baking Powder.

Sprinkle With Cinnamon And Sugar And Bake In Dripping Pan.

Mrs. W. H. Faulds.

White Cake.

Put In Teacup The Whites Of Two Eggs. Add Enough Soft Butter To Half Fill The Cup And Fill Brim Full With Milk.

Put In A Sieve: 1cup Sugar.

1 ½ Cups Flour.

1 Rounded Teaspoon Baking Powder.

Sift These Into Mixing Bowl, Empty Contents Of Teacup Into Dry Ingredients And Beat Briskly Five Minutes Flavor And Bake In Moderate Oven. Ice With Boiled Icing.

Mrs. E. E. Buckman.

Lake Cakes.

2 Cups Flour.

½ Teaspoon Soda Dissolved In Sour Cream.

3 Eggs (Whites For Icing).

½ Cup Butter.	1 Teaspoon Cloves.
½ Cup Sugar.	½ Cup Molasses.
1 Cup Sour Cream	

Mrs. T. L. Welles.

Measured Pound Cake.

1 ½ Cups Butter.	1 Teaspoon Baking Powder.
2 ½ Cups Flour, Heaped.	2 Cups Sugar.

2 Tablespoons Hot Water Added Last.

7 Eggs, Whites And Yolks, Beaten Separately.

Mrs. H. B. Payne.

Loaf Cake.

3 Cups Light Bread Dough.	2 Cups Sugar.
1 Cup Butter.	4 Eggs.
1 Cup Raisins Chopped Fine.	1 Teaspoon Soda.

Nutmeg, Cinnamon, Cloves.

Miss Raub.

Hickory-Nut Cake.

1 ½ Cups Sugar.
½ Cup Butter.
¾ Cup Cold Water.
2 Cups Flour.

Whites Of Four Eggs.
1 Teaspoon Baking Powder.
1 Large Cup Chopped Nuts

Mrs. Phillip Hessel.

Nut And Cracker Cake.

1 ½ Cups Sugar.
½ Cup Butter.
7 Eggs.
Crumbs.
4 Tablespoons Milk.
½ Cup Chopped Raisins.

½ Cup Chopped Citron.
1 Cup Grated Chocolate.
1 ½ Cups Fine Cracker

½ Cup Chopped Walnuts.

Bake In Large Tin In Moderate Oven One Hour.

Mrs. Franck.

Hickory-Nut Cake.

2 Cups Sugar.
1 Cup Butter.
1 Cup Milk.
3 Cups Flour.

2 Cups Nuts.
4 Eggs.
3 Teaspoons Baking Powder.

Bake Until A Straw Comes Out Clean. Don't Have Oven Too Hot.

Mrs. A. E. Miller.

Cinnamon Cake.

1 Cup Sugar.
2 Eggs.
Good Sized Piece Of Butter.

1 Cup Sweet Milk.
3 Cups Flour.
2 Teaspoons Baking Powder.

Save White Of One Egg For Top.

Top.
1 Cup Sugar.
White Of One Egg.

Butter Size Of Egg.
1 Spoon Cinnamon.

Spread On Cake And Bake.

English Walnut Cake (With Maple Icing).

2 Cups Granulated Sugar.

2 Heaping Teaspoons Baking Powder.

1 Cup Butter.   1 Cup Milk.

3 Scant Cups Flour.   7 Eggs (Whites.)

Orange Or Vanilla Flavoring.

Cream Butter And Sugar Very Light. Add Little Milk, Then Little Flour, Continuing Until All Have Been Used. Bake In Three Tins.

Icing.

2 Cakes Maple Sugar.   Whites Of 2 Eggs.

1/4 Lbs. English Walnuts.   Pinch Cream Tartar.

Boil Maple Syrup With Cream TartarIn Boiling Water Enough To Cover Until It Will Form A Soft Ball In Cold Water. Pour On Beaten Whites And Beat Until It Forms A Thick Soft Cream. Put With Chopped Nuts Between Layers Of Cake.

Miss Helen Goodwin.

Sponge Cake.

1 Cup Sugar.   4 Tablespoons Water.

1 Cup Flour.   2 Teaspoons Baking Powder.

3 Eggs.   1 Teaspoon Lemon Extract.

Beat Yolks Of Eggs With Lemon And Half The Water Until Very Light. Beat, Beat, Beat. Add Remainder Of Water, Flour With Baking Powder And Beaten Whites. Bake Until The Cake Loosens From Pan.

Mrs. Franck.

Delicate Cake.

1 Cup Butter.   3 ½ Cups Flour Well Sifted.

2 Cups Sugar.   1 Cup Milk.

2 Teaspoons Baking Powder In Last Cup Of Flour. Whites Of 10 Eggs, Well Beaten.

Stir Whites In Lightly Last Of All. Tiny Slices Of Citron Mixed Through This Cake Make It Very Nice And Keep It Fresh A Week Or More. A Fine Recipe From Boston.

Pork Cake.

12 Oz. Pork Chopped Fine.   1 Lb. Raisins
Chopped.
Pt. Boiling Water.   1 Teaspoon Soda.
   Cups Sugar.   8 Cups Flour.
1 1 Cup Molasses.
1 Teaspoon Each, Cloves, Cinnamon And Nutmeg.
   Pour Boiling Water On Pork And Let Stand Until
Cool Enough To Mix.   Add Other Ingredients.

Mrs. Brewster.

Roll Jelly Cake

3 Eggs.   1 Teaspoon Cream Tartar.
1 Cup Sugar.   ½ Teaspoon Soda (Small.)
1 Cup Flour.
   Bake Quickly In Large Pan. Roll With Jelly While Hot.

Mrs. W. L. Dean.

Sand Tarts.

½ Cup Butter.   ½ Teaspoon Baking Powder.
½ Cup Milk (Scant.)   Pinch Of Salt.
1 Cup Sugar.   A Scrape Of Nutmeg.
1 ½ Cups Flour.
   Roll Thin.

Molasses Cake.

2 Cups Molasses.   1 Tablespoon Soda,
1 Cup Sugar.   1 Cup Sour Milk.
2 Lemons.   Salt, Ginger.
2 Eggs.   ½ Cup Lard.

Mrs. Newitt.

Connecticut Loaf Cake.

1 Cup Yeast.
1 Cup Sugar.
3 Cups New Milk.
   Flour To Make Batter Stiffer Than Cake, But Not As Stiff

As Bread.

Let Rise In Warm Place During Night. In Morning Cream:

1/2 Cup Butter.   3 Cups Sugar.

2 Cups Lard.   1 Egg. Well Beaten.

Knead Into This Mixture The Risen Dough. Add:

2 Cups Chopped Citron.   1 Nutmeg, Grated.

1 Tablespoon Mace.   Wine Glass Brandy.

2 Cups Seeded Raisins Dredged In Flour.

Let Rise Again, And, Last Of All, Add Pinch Of Soda In Spoonful Of Flour.

Miss M. C. Tubbs.

Checker-Board Cake.

2 Cups A Sugar.   3 ½ Cups Flour.

3 Eggs.   2 ½ Teaspoons Baking Powder.

½ Cup Butter.

Keep White Of One Egg For Icing.

1 Cup Milk.

Divide Dough Into Two Equal Parts. Stir Tablespoon Of Melted Chocolate Into One Part. Take Three Cake Tins And In The Middle Of Two Put A Teaspoon Of Dark Mixture; In The Third, A Teaspoon Of Light. Around The Dark Centers Put Row Of Light Mixture; Around Light Center, A Row Of Dark. Put Four Rows In Each Tin. When Baked Put Layer With Light Center Between Layers With Dark Center.

Icing.

Beat White Of One Egg. Stiffen With Powdered Sugar, Add Spoonful Melted Chocolate.

Nellie Grover.

Myrtle Cake.

1 Cup Sugar.   1 Egg.

2/3 Cup Water.   Pinch Of Salt.

2 Cups Flour.   2 Tablespoons Baking Powder.

1 Tablespoon Butter.

Mrs. T. D. Hutchings.

Tilden Cake.

1 Cup Butter.
2 Cups Powdered Sugar.
1 Cup Sweet Milk.
3 Cups Flour.
½ Cup Corn Starch.

4 Eggs.
2 Teaspoons Baking Powder.
2 Teaspoons Lemon Extract.

Miss Lawley.

Reading Sponge Cake.

5 Eggs (Whites Of Two For Icing.) 2 Cups Flour.
2 Teaspoons Baking Powder. 2 Cups Powdered Sugar.
Rind And Juice Of One Orange. ½ Cup Cold Water..
   Bake In Layers With White Icing.
Mrs. Franck.

Sponge Cake.

6 Eggs. ½ Lb. Flour.
¾ Lb. Granulated Sugar. 1 Gill Water.
   Beat Yolks Of Eggs Very Light. Add Well-Beaten Whites. Boil Sugar And Water Until Clear, And Pour Into Beaten Eggs. Beat Until Cold. Add Juice Of One Lemon And The Flour.
Mrs. W. H. Faulds.

Sponge Cake.

3 Eggs. 1 Teaspoon Baking Powder.
Salt. 1 Teaspoon Vanilla,
1 Cup Sugar. ½ Cup Boiling Water,
1 Cup Flour.
   Beat Eggs With Salt Five Minutes. Add Sugar And Beat Again. Sift Baking Powder Through Flour And Stir In Water Last.
Mrs. Hilbert.

Phoebe Nut Cake

1 Cup Butter. Whites Of Eight Eggs.
2 Cups Sugar. 4 Cups Flour,

3 Teaspoons Baking Powder.   2 Cups Hickory Nut Meats.
1 Cup Sweet Milk.

Butternut Cake.

1 Cup Sugar.
2 Teaspoons Cinnamon.
½ Cup Butter.
2 Cups Flour (More If Needed.)
1 Cup Buttermilk Or Sour Milk.   A Little Nutmeg.
2 Eggs.
2 Cups Butter-Nut Meats.
1 Small Teaspoon Soda.

Miss Parry.

Hickory-Nut Cake.

2 Cups Sugar.   2 Teaspoons Baking Powder,
1 Cup Butter.   1 Teaspoon Vanilla.
1 Cup Milk.   1/4 Cups Chopped Hickory Nut
Meats.
3 Cups Flour.
Whites Of Four And One Whole Egg.

Mrs. D. H. Eavenson.

Nut Cake

1 Cup Butter.   3 Cups Flour.
2cups Sugar.   2 Teaspoons Baking Powder.
4 Eggs.   2 Cups Chopped Nuts.
1 Cup Water.
Icing.
    Boil Three Cups Sugar In One Cup Water Until It Hairs.
Whip Slowly Into Whites Of Eggs.

Mrs. H. C. Smythe.

Imperial Cake.

1 Lb. Butter.   ¾ Lb. Citron.
1 Lb. Sugar.   ¾ Lb. Jordan Almonds.
1 Lb. Flour.   12 Eggs.
1 Lb. Raisins.
Add Wine Glass Of Brandy If You Wish To Keep Some

Time.

Miss Elizabeth Loveland.

Imperial Cake.

1 Lb. Butter.
1 Lb. Sugar.
1 Lb. Flour.
2 Lbs. Almonds.
2 Lbs. Raisins.

¾ Lb. Citron.
12 Eggs.
1 Nutmeg.
1 Lemon.
2 Teaspoons Baking Powder:

Mrs. Pierce Butler.

Lady Cake.

1 Cup Butter.
2 Cups Sugar.
1 Cup Sweet Milk.
Whites Of Eight Eggs

4 Cups Flour.
1 Teaspoon Soda.
2 Teaspoons Cream Tartar.
Almonds To Flavor.

Miss Esther French.

White Layer Cake.

1 Cup Butter.
2 Cups Sugar.
Powder.
1 Cup Sweet Milk.

Whites Of Five Eggs Beaten Stiff.
2 Heaping Teaspoons Baking

3 Cups Flour.

Mrs. Hammond Talbot.

Queen Cake.

2 Cups Sugar.
1 Cup Butter.
1 Cup Sweet Milk.
4 Cups Flour.

1 Lb. Raisins And Citron Together.
½ Lb. Almonds.
A Few Currants.
Small Wine Glass Brandy.

8 Eggs, Yolks And Whites Beaten Separately.
   Dust Raisins With Part Of Measured Flour.

Miss Raub

Lemon Cake.

3 Cups Sugar.
1 Cup Butter.
1 Cup Milk.

1 Teaspoon Soda Dissolved In Milk.
Juice And Rind Of One Lemon.
4 Cups Flour.

5 Eggs, Yolks And Whites Beaten Separately.

Miss Jessie Macfarlane.

Snickerdoodle.

2 Eggs.
½ Cup Butter.
2 Cups Sugar.
1 Cup Milk.

3 Level Cups Flour.
2 Teaspoons Cream Tartar.
1 Teaspoon Soda.
½ Teaspoon Salt.

Cream Butter And Sugar Together. Add Beaten Whites, Then Yolks. Dissolve Soda In Milk. Mix Cream Tartar And Salt With Flour. Sift Cinnamon And Sugar Over The Cake And Bake Twenty Minutes In Flat Biscuit Tins In Moderate Oven.   Cut In Squares When Cold.

Mrs. W. F. Church.

Spice Cake.

3 Eggs, Yolks And Whites Beaten Separately.
1 Teaspoon Each Cinnamon, Cloves And Nutmeg,
¾ Cup Butter.
2 Cups Sugar.
1 Cup Strong Coffee.

1 Teaspoon Cream Tartar.
½ Teaspoon Soda.
Flour.

Nellie Grover.

White Citron Cake.

1 Cup Butter.
3 Cups Sugar.
4 Cups Flour.
1 Cup Sweet Milk.

Whites Of Eight Eggs.
1 Teaspoon Soda.
2 Teaspoons Cream Tartar.

Grated Rind And Juice Of One Lemon.
½ Lb. Citron Sliced Fine.
Juice Of Lemon May Be Left Out.

Mrs. T. H. B. Lewis.

Jackson Cake.

8 Eggs.
I Lb. Powdered Sugar.
   Bake In Moderate Oven.

½ Lb. Butter.
¾ Cup Flour.

Mrs. D. M. Rosser.

Dolly Varden Cake.

2 Cups Sugar.

3 Eggs.

114

2/3 Cup Butter.   1 Teaspoon Cream
Tartar.
1 Cup Sweet Milk.   ½ Teaspoon Soda.
3 Cups Flour.   Flavor With Lemon.

  Bake One-Half The Above Mixture In Two Pans. To The
Remainder Add:
1 Tablespoon Molasses.
1 Teaspoon Each Cinnamon, Cloves, Nutmeg And
Allspice.
1 Cup Chopped Raisins.
Piece Of Citron Chopped Fine
½ Cup Currants.
  Put Together With Jelly Or Icing.

                                         Mrs. Brewster.

Spice Cake.

2 Cups Brown Sugar.   4 Cups Flour.
1 Cup Butter And Lard.   1 Lb. Stewed Raisins.
1 Cup Sour Milk.   1 Teaspoon Each Cinnamon
Cloves And Nutmeg.
2 Teaspoons Soda.   3 Eggs.
  Put Soda In Sour Milk.

                                         Mrs. E. R. Morgan.

Coffee Cake.

1 Cup Sugar.   1 ¼ Teaspoons Soda.
1 Cup Butter.   1 Teaspoon Cloves.
2 Eggs.   1 Nutmeg.
1 Cup Cold Coffee.   A Little Ginger.
1 Cup Molasses.   1 Lb. Each Raisins And
Currants.
3 Cups Flour.   2 Teaspoons Baking Powder.
                                         Mrs. H. B. Payne.

Coffee Cake.

Cup Lard And Butter Mixed.   1 Cup Raisins.
2 Eggs.   1 Cup Currants.
1 Cup Cold Coffee.   3 ½ Cups Flour.
1 Cup Sugar.   1 Teaspoon Soda

½ Cup Molasses.   Spices To Taste

Mrs. H. G. Ellis.

Mountain Cake.

2 Eggs, Whites And Yolks Beaten Separately.

2 Cups Flour.   1 Teaspoon Cream Tartar.

1 Cup Sugar.   ½ Teaspoon Soda.

½ Cup Butter.   1 Teaspoon Lemon Extract.

½ Cup Sweet Milk.

Beat Butter Light Before Adding Sugar.

Mrs. Brewster.

Two Egg Cake.

1 Cup Sugar.   2 Cups Flour.

½ Cup Butter.

1 Teaspoon Soda Dissolved In Little Hot Water,

1 Cup Sweet Milk.

2 Teaspoons Cream Tartar. Vanilla.

2 Eggs, Yolks And Whites Beaten Separately.

Mix Cream Tartar In One-Half Cup Of The Flour. Bake In Two Layers.

Mrs. James H. Hughes.

Angel Cake.

Whites Of Eight Large Or Nine Small Eggs.

1 1/4 Cups Sugar Measured After Sifting Five Times.

A Trifle Over One Cup Flour, Measured After Sifting Five Times.

Scant One-Half Teaspoon Cream Tartar.

Add Pinch Salt To Eggs Before Whipping.

Whip Eggs To Foam, Add Cream Tartar And Whip Until Very Stiff. Beat In Sugar And Flavoring. Fold Flour Lightly Through. Put In Moderate Oven At Once And Bake From Twenty To Forty Minutes.

Mrs. T. R. Phillips.

Angel's Food.

1 ½ Tumblers Powdered Sugar.

Whites Of Ten Eggs Beaten To Stiff Froth.

1 Tumbler Flour.

Flavor With Vanilla Or Rosewater.

1 Teaspoon Cream Tartar.

Beat Cream Tartar With Eggs. Sift Sugar And Flour Together And Stir Gently Into The Eggs. Bake In An Un-Greased Pan Forty Minutes.

Miss Raub.

Cheap Black Chocolate Cake.

1 Cup Sugar.	½ Teaspoon Soda Dissolved In Milk.
1 Egg.	1 ½ Cups Flour.
1 Tablespoon Butter.	3 Squares Chocolate.
1 Cup Milk.	1 Teaspoon Baking Powder

Beat Yolk Of Egg With Sugar And Add Flour. Melt Chocolate And Butter Together And Add Last. Use White Of Egg For Icing. Don't Use More Flour. Bake In Two Layers.

Mrs. James H. Hughes.

Sunshine Cake.

1 Cup Flour (Scant) Measured After Sifting Five Times.

Whites Of Seven Eggs.

Yolks Of Five Eggs.

1 Cup Sugar.

1 Teaspoon Orange Extract.

1 Teaspoon Cream Tartar.

Beat The Whites Very Stiff With The Cream Tartar And A Pinch Of Salt. Add Sugar, Beat Thoroughly. Add Flavoring And The Yolks Beaten Very Thick; Beat Lightly And Carefully Stir In The Flour. Bake In Tube Pan In Moderate Oven Forty Or Fifty Minutes.

Miss Raub.

Apple Sauce Cake.

1 Cup Sugar.	1 Cup Raisins.
½ Cup Butter.	2 Teaspoons Soda.
2 Cups Flour.	1 ½ Cups Apple
Sauce.	

1 Teaspoon Each Cloves, Cinnamon And Nutmeg.

Bake In Two Pans In Moderate Oven One And One-

Quarter Hours.

Mrs. Geo. H. Ives.

Cocoanut Cake.

2 Eggs.	2 Teaspoons Cream Tartar.
1 Cup Sweet Milk(Large.)	½ Cup Shortening (Scant.)
1 Teaspoon Soda.	Flour.
Flavor With Lemon.	

Gold Cake.

½ Cup Butter.	3 Cups Flour.
2 Cups Sugar.	1 Very Small Teaspoon Soda.
1 Cup Milk.	2 Very Small Teaspoons Cream Tartar.
Yolks Of Five Eggs.	

Miss Augusta Hoyt.

Gold Cake.

1 Cup Butter.	½ Cup Sweet Milk.
1 Cup Sugar.	2 Teaspoons Baking Powder
Yolks Of 8 Eggs.	1 ½ Cups Flour.

Mix In Order Given. Beat Yolks Thoroughly Before Adding To Butter And Sugar. Beat Cake Hard Before Putting Into Pan. Bake In Tube Pan Forty Minutes. Makes Good Layer Cake.

Tilden Cake.

1 Cup Butter.	3 Cups Flour.
2 Cups Powdered Sugar.	½ Cup Corn Starch.
4 Eggs Beaten Light.	
2 Tablespoons Vanilla Or Lemon,	
1 Cup Sweet Milk.	

Sift Cornstarch And Flour Well.

Mrs. W. L. Stewart.

Gold Loaf.

¾ Cup Butter.	2 1/3 Cups Flour.
2/3 Cup Sweet Milk.	1 Teaspoon Cream Tartar.
½ Teaspoon Soda.	1 ¼ Cups Sugar (Sift After

Measuring.)

Vanilla.

Sift Flour, Measure, Add Soda And Sift Three Times. Beat Yolks About Half, Add Cream Tartar And Beat Until Stiff. Beat All Together Very Hard, Put In Oven At Once And Bake From Three To Five Hours.

Mrs. T. R. Phillips.

Bread Cake.

3 Large Cups Raised Dough. The Firmer, The Better.

4 Eggs.	1 Teaspoon Soda.
2 Cups Sugar.	Spice And Fruit.
1 Cup Butter.	½ Cup Buttermilk Or Sour Milk.

Add Flour If Too Thin.

Mrs. Von Krug.

Bread Cake.

3 Cups Very Light Dough.

1 Teaspoon Soda Dissolved In Hot Water.

3 Cups Brown Sugar.	3 Eggs.
1 Lb. Raisins.	1 Cup Butter.

1 Nutmeg Grated.

Mix Butter And Sugar Together, Add Eggs And Nutmeg, Beat Well And Mix All Thoroughly With Dough. Beat Very Light.   Let Rise Again Before Baking.   Makes Two Loaves.

Miss Frances Dorrance.

Bread Cake.

3 Cups Light Bread Dough.	1 Teaspoon Soda.
2 ½ Cups Sugar.	1 Teaspoon Cinnamon.
3 Eggs.	½ Teaspoon Cloves.
1 Cup Butter.	½ Teaspoon Nutmeg Grated.

Use More Spice If Desired.

Mrs. Geo. Shoemaker.

The "Bully" Chocolate Cake.

½ Cup Butter.

4 Egg, Yolks And Whites Beaten Separately.

½ Cup Sugar.   1 Heaping Teaspoon Baking Powder.
½ Cup Milk.   1 ¾ Cups Flour.
     Add Well Beaten Yolks To Creamed Butter And Sugar. Add Milk And 2 Oz. Baker's Chocolate Dissolved In Five Tablespoons Boiling Water. Add Stiffly Beaten Whites Last. Bake In Layers.

Filling.

½ Pt. Cream.

½ Cake Baker's Chocolate.

     Melt Chocolate Over Kettle Of Boiling Water. Add As Many Teaspoons Of Confectioner's Sugar As You Have Of Cream.   Beat Until Perfectly Smooth.

.H. W. T.

Chocolate Cake.

1 ¼ Cups Sugar.   3 Teaspoons Baking Powder.

¼ Cup Butter.

½ Cake Chocolate Dissolved In ½ Cup Boiling Water.

2 Eggs.   2 Cups Flour.

½ Cup Sweet Milk.   Flavor To Taste.

Put Chocolate In Last.

Mrs. J. G. Sperling.

Black Chocolate Cake.

Boil Together:

½ Cup Milk.   1 Egg Beaten.

1/3 Cake Grated Chocolate.   2 Tablespoons Boiling Water.

When Cold Add:

1 Cup Sugar.   2 Cups Flour.

½ Cup Butter.   2 Teaspoons Baking Powder.

½ Cup Milk.

2 Eggs, Yolks And Whites Beaten Separately.

    Add Whites Of Eggs Last.

Nellie Grover.

Cup Pound Cake.

1 ½   Cups Flour.   ½ Teaspoon Soda.

1 ½ Cups Sugar.   5 Eggs.

1 Cup Butter.

Beat Butter And Flour To A Cream. Add Eggs And Sugar. Baking Powder Last.

Mrs. Meginess.

Silver Cake.

3 Cups Sugar.	¼ Lb- Citron, Cut Fine.
1 Cup Butter.	1 Teaspoon Cream Tartar.
1 Cup Milk.	¼ Teaspoon Soda.
4 ½ Cups Flour.	Whites Of Ten Eggs.

Miss Jessie Macfarlane.

Pound Cake.

1 Lb. Sugar.	10 Eggs.
1 Lb. Flour.	Wine Glass Of Brandy.
¾ Lb. Butter.	

Miss Jessie Macfarlane.

Sponge Cake.

3 Eggs, Thoroughly Beaten.	1 Cup Sugar.
1 Cup Flour.	4 Tablespoons Water.

Boil Water And Sugar Together And Pour Gradually Over Eggs. Flavor With Lemon.

Miss Jessie Macfarlane.

Orange Cake.

2 Cups Sugar.	½ Teaspoon Soda.
½ Cup Butter (Scant).	1 Teaspoon Cream Tartar.
2 Cups Flour.	Rind Of One Orange.
½ Cup Water.	Juice Of One And One-Half

Oranges.

Yolks of 5 Eggs.	Whites Of 4 Eggs.

Beat Butter To Cream, Add Sugar Gradually, Then The Orange, The Eggs Well Beaten, The Water, And The Flour In Which Soda And Cream Tartar Have Been Mixed.

Icing.

White Of One Egg. 1 ½ Cups Or More Of Powdered Sugar.

Juice Of One And One-Half Oranges.

Mrs. George W. Lewis.

Huckleberry Cake.

½ Cup Butter.   1 Tablespoon Soda.
1 ½ Cups Sour Milk.   Salt.
½ Cup Molasses.   Huckleberries To Taste
1 Cup Sugar.   Flour To Make Stiff Batter.
2 Eggs.

    To Be Eaten Hot With Butter Or As A Pudding With Sauce.

                    Mrs. H. H. Welles.

Coffee Cake.

1 Cup Strong, Cold Coffee.   1 Teaspoon Allspice.
1 Cup Sugar.   Cinnamon.
1 Cup Butter.   1 Teaspoon Soda Dissolved
In Little Vinegar.
1 Cup Molasses.   1 Lb. Raisins.
4 Cups Flour.   1 Lb. Currants.
3 Eggs.   ½ Lb. Citron.
2 Nutmegs.   2 Teaspoons Cloves.
    Bake Slowly.

                    Mrs. George F. Lee.

Chocolate Caramel Cake.

1 Cup Sugar.   ½ Cup Sweet Milk.
½ Cake Chocolate.   Yolk Of 1 Egg.
    Boil Until Thick, Then Cool.

Cake Part.

I Cup Sugar.   3 Cups Flour (Pastry).
2/3 Cup Butter.   2 Teaspoons Baking Powder.
1 Cup Sweet Milk.   1 Teaspoon Vanilla.
2 Eggs.

    Put Together Before Putting In Flour. Bake In Three Layers. Use White Frosting.

                    Mrs. F. W. Frantz.

Edinborough Ginger Bread.

4 Cups Flour.   2 Eggs.
2 Cups Sugar.   4 Tablespoons Drippings.

2 Cups Fine Oat Meal.

2 Cups Molasses.

1 Cup Warm Water.

¼ Lb. Orange Peel.

2 Tablespoons Ginger.

2 Tablespoons Soda.

½ Lb. Blanched Almonds.

Split Almonds And Chop Orange Peel.

Mrs. George W. Lewis.

Molasses Cake.

2 Eggs.

2 Cups Molasses.

1 Cup Sour Milk.

Don't Mix Too Stiff.

2 Teaspoons Soda (Small).

Nutmeg.

Salt.

Mrs. John Nugent.

Boston Gingerbread.

2 Small Tablespoons Soda Dissolved In Boiling Water.

I Lb. Butter.

1 Heaping Tablespoon
ginger.

1 Lb. Sugar.

1 Even Tablespoon Cinnamon.

1 Pt. Molasses.

1 Pt. Sour Cream Or
buttermilk.

2 ½ Lbs. Flour.

½ Teaspoon Cloves (Scant).

This Makes Five Or Six Small Loaves.

Miss Augusta Hoyt.

Ginger Cake.

½ Cup N. O. Molasses.

½ Cup Sugar.

½ Cup Lard.

½ Cup Sour Milk Or Hot Water.

Cinnamon.

1 Egg.

1 Teaspoon Soda.

1 Teaspoon Ginger.

1 Teaspoon

Miss Jessie Macfarlane.

Gossamer Gingerbread.

½ Cup Butter.   2 Cups Flour (Scant).
1 Cup Sugar.   1 Egg.
½ Cup Sweet Milk.   1 ½ Tablespoons Ginger.

Spread As Thin As Possible On Well Buttered Tin Sheets. Bake In Moderate Oven. When Baked Cut In Narrow Strips And Take Off Tin While Hot.

Miss Elizabeth Loveland.

Soft Ginger Cake.

1 Cup Molasses.
½ Teaspoon Ginger.
2 Tablespoons Lard.
1 Teaspoon Cinnamon.
1 Cup Hot Water.
2 Cups Flour.
1 Teaspoon Soda In The Hot Water.
Salt.

Mrs. C. Bach.

Crullers, Doughnuts, Etc.

Bixby Doughnuts.

2 Cups Sugar.   3 Eggs.
1 Cup Sweet Milk.   3 Teaspoons Baking Powder.
1 Large Tablespoon Melted Butter.
Mix Into Soft Dough And Fry In Deep Fat.

Mrs. C. W. Bixby.

Crullers.

3 Cups Sugar.   1 Pt. Buttermilk.
½ Cup Butter.   1 Teaspoon Soda.
3 Eggs.

Miss Jessie Macfarlane.

Crullers.

5 Eggs.   2 Cups Milk.
3 Cups Sugar.   2 Qts. Flour.

1 Heaping Tablespoon Butter.   2 Teaspoons
Baking Powder,

                              Mrs. Geo. H. Ives.

Cream Fried Cakes.
1 Coffee Cup Sour Cream,Not Too Rich.,
2 Eggs—One Will Do.   2 Teaspoons Salt.
1 Coffee Cup Sugar.   1 Teaspoon Soda.
Mix With Flour, Roll And Fry.

                              Mrs. Geo. Shoemaker.

German Crullers.
2 Eggs.   1 Cup Milk.
1 Tablespoon Lard.   1 Teaspoon Baking Powder.
1 Cup Sugar.   Flour To Make Soft Dough.
   Knead Lightly.   When Cold Dust With Powdered
Sugar.

                       Mrs. E. R. Morgan.

Puff Doughnuts.
3 Eggs.
Nutmeg.
1 Cup Sugar.
2 Heaping Teaspoons Baking Powder.
1 Pt. Milk.
Salt.
   Flour Enough To Permit The Spoon To Stand
Upright In Mixture.
   Beat Until Very Light. Drop Dessert Spoonfuls
Into Boiling Lard.
These Are Not Rich And Do Not Absorb Fat.

                    Mrs. E. G. Gage.

Doughnuts.
2 Cups Sugar.   2 Eggs.
2 Cups Milk.   1 Tablespoon Soda.
2 Tablespoons Butter. 1 Tablespoon Brandy.
2 Tablespoons Cream Tartar.   Flour To Roll.

Mix Butter And Cream Tartar Together. After Cutting Out Let Stand One Hour Before Cooking. Mrs. Wm. Mccolloch.

Fried Cakes.

1 Cup Sugar.
1 Cup Buttermilk.
3 Tablespoons Melted Butter.
Flour To Make Firm Dough, Ter.
2 Eggs.
1 Teaspoon Soda.

Mix Sugar And Eggs Together. Add Buttermilk, Flour, Butter, And Soda Dissolved In Little Of The Milk.
Mrs. Albert E. Miller.

Crullers Without Sugar.

1 Qt. Flour.
3 Teaspoons Baking Powder.
Butter.
Milk to Make Quite Soft.
1 Teaspoon Salt.
1 Level Tablespoon

Cut In Strips, Twist Into Crullers And Fry.
Mrs. W. L. Foster.

Poplar Chips.

1 pt. Thick, Sweet Cream.
1 Teaspoon Salt.
4 Eggs, Yolks And Whites Beaten Separately.
Flour To Roll—Not Too Much.
Cut In Strips And Fry Like Doughnuts.
Mrs. Markle.

Doughnuts.

1 Cup Sugar.
Flour.
3 Tablespoons Melted Lard.
Baking Powder.
1 Small Teaspoon Salt.
1 Cup Sweet Milk.
5 Small Cups

3 Even Teaspoons

2 Or 3 Eggs.
A Little Nutmeg.

Add Eggs To Sugar Without Beating, Then Salt, Melted Lard From Kettle And Other Ingredients. Mix As Soft As Possible. Fry In Hot Fat.

Mrs. Hassiby.

Raised Doughnuts.

In The Afternoon Make A Sponge With:

1 Cup Sugar.   ½ Yeast Cake
1/2 Cup Sweet Milk.   ½ Cup Cold Water.
½ Cup Boiling Water.   Salt.
½ Cup Mashed Potatoes.   Flour To Make Soft Sponge.
1/3 Cup Lard.

At Bedtime Add:

2 Eggs.   Flour Enough To Form Into Lump
½ Teaspoon Salt.   Nutmeg.

In Morning Roll, Cut Out And Let Stand Until Very Light. Fry In Hot Lard.

Ginger Snaps, Etc.

Ginger Snaps.

Boil Together Fifteen Minutes:

1 Pt. Molasses.
2 ½ Cup Water.

While Boiling Stir In One Cup Butter Or Lard, Or A Mixture Of The Two.

When Cold Add :—

2 Teaspoons Soda, A Little Ginger And Salt.
Flour To Roll.

Miss Lawley.

Ginger Cakes.

2 Cups N. O. Molasses.
2 Eggs.
1/2 Cup Sugar.
2 Teaspoons Soda Dissolved In Milk.

1 Cup Butter.
2 Teaspoons Ginger
½ Cup Buttermilk Or Sour Milk.
Roll As Soft As Possible.

Miss Jessie Macfarlane.

Ginger Cookies.

1 Cup Molasses.   2 Teaspoons Soda,
1 Cup Brown Sugar. 2 Teaspoons Ginger,
1 Cup Melted Shortening.
Salt.   ½ Cup Hot Water.
Flour To Roll Out.

Ginger Cakes.

1 Cup Brown Sugar.   1 Tablespoon Soda.
1 Cup Lard.
Ginger, Nutmeg, Cinnamon To Taste
1 Cup Hot Water.   Flour To Stiffen.
1 Egg.   1 ½ Cups N. O. Molasses.
Drop By Spoonfuls Into Well Greased Pan.

Mrs. Grover.

Ginger Snaps.

1 Cup Molasses.   ½ Teaspoon Soda,
1 Cup Butter.   ½ Teaspoon Ginger
½ Cup Granulated Sugar.
Boil the Ingredients Five Minutes. Cool, Mix In
Flour Till Very Stiff, Roll Very Thin And Bake In
Moderate Oven.

Miss Elizabeth Loveland.

Ginger Cookies With Frosting.

1 Cup Butter Or Lard.   ½ Cup Sour Milk.
1 Cup Sugar.   1 Teaspoon Ginger.
1 Cups Molasses.   1 Teaspoon Cinnamon.
3 Eggs (Whites For Frosting.
4 Teaspoons Soda (Scant),
1/2 Teaspoon Salt.

Roll One-Fourth Inch Thick. Have Dough Stiff Enough To Be Taken Up With Knife.

Frosting.

One Large Cup Sugar Boiled With Four Spoonfuls Water Until It Threads.

Stir Into Whites Of Eggs, Beat Well And Spread Over Cookies.

Mrs. J. R. Davis.

Orange Ginger Snaps.

1 Qt. Molasses.	1 Teaspoon Cloves.
1 Lb. Sugar.	Grated Rind Of Two Large Oranges
¾ Lb. Butter.	½ Lb. Lard.
½ Teacup Brandy.	1 Oz Cinnamon.
4 Lbs. Flour.	2 Oz. Ginger.

Boil Molasses, Sugar, Butter And Lard Together, Add Other Ingredients And Let Stand Until Next Day. Roll Thin And Bake In Moderate Oven.

Mrs. Fancourt.

Ginger Snaps.

2 Cups Boiled Molasses.	1 Egg.
I Cup Sugar.	1 Tablespoon Ginger,
1 Cup Lard.	1 Tablespoon Soda.
1 Cup Buttermilk.	

Mrs. Meginess.

Ginger Cookies.

1 Cup Molasses.	2 ½ Cups Flour.
½ Cup Lard.	1 Tablespoon Ginger.
½ Cup Water.	1 Heaping Teaspoon Soda.
1 Egg.	1 Scant Teaspoon Salt.

Drop In Well-Greased Pans. Bake In Hot Oven.

Mrs. L. C. Diggory.

Mrs. Conover's Ginger Snaps.

1 Pt. Butter Or Lard.	1 Tablespoon Cinnamon.
1 Pt. Molasses.	½ Tablespoon Allspice,

1 Cup Sugar.   ½ Tablespoon Cloves.
½ Teaspoon Salt.   1 Tablespoon Soda In Half
1 Nutmeg, Grated.   Cup Boiling Water.
   1 Tablespoon Ginger.
            Flour To Roll Out.

                                   Mrs. Geo. Shoemaker.

Ginger Snaps.
1 Cup Butter.
1 Cup Sugar.
1 Cup Molasses.
1 Egg.
Flour To Make Very Stiff.
1 Even Teaspoon Soda And 2 Teaspoons Ginger
Mixed With 1 Tablespoon Hot Water.

                                   Mrs. T. R. Phillips.

Liebe Kuchen.
1 Qt. Molasses.   2 Teaspoon Soda.
1 Qt. Flour.   1 Cup Lard Or Butter.
1 Lemon.   2 Teaspoons Soda.
1 Large Teaspoon Each, Allspice, Cloves, Cinnamon,
Nutmeg And Ginger.

   Boil Molasses. Add Other Ingredients And Keep In
Warm Place Twenty-Four Hours. Work The Dough An
Hour. Roll And Bake Like Ginger Snaps, Putting Icing And
Thin Piece Of Citron On Each Cake. They May Also Be Cut
In Rectangular Shape.

                                   Mrs. Franck

Cookies, Jumbles, Etc.

Charlotte Russe.
¼ Package Gelatine, Dissolved In Very Little Water.
1 Pt. Whipped Cream, Flavored And Sweetened To
Taste.

Stir Gelatine Into Cream. Line A Mold With Lady
Fingers And Pour Cream Over.

Fruit Cookies.

2 Eggs.
1 Teaspoon Soda Dissolved In Tablespoon Water,
1 ½ Cups Sugar.
1 Cup Butter.   *
1 Teaspoon Each Cloves, Cinnamon And Nutmeg,
1 Cup Chopped Raisins Or Currants.
Flour To Stiffen.

Miss Esther French.

Rocks.

2 Lbs. English Walnuts 1lb. Shelled).   3 Eggs.
1 Lb. Chopped Raisins.   Salt.
1 ½ Cups Sugar.   1 Cup Butter.
3 Cups Flour.   1 Wine Glass Wine Or
Brandy.
1 Teaspoon Soda Dissolved In Hot Water.

Moravian Christmas Cakes.

1Lb. Sugar.   ½ Spoon Cinnamon.
5 Oz. Butter.   2 Tablespoons Rose Water.
4 Eggs.   1 1/ Lbs. Flour.
   Mix Flour, Butter And Sugar Together. Beat Eggs
Well. Roll Out Thin.
Miss Esther French.

Swedish Cookies.

2 Cups Sugar.   2 Teaspoons Baking
Powder.
1 ½ Cups Butter.   1 Teaspoon Vanilla.
3 Eggs.
   Flour To Make Soft Dough. Roll Thin And
Sprinkle With Chopped Nuts And Sugar.

Mrs. T. L. Welles.

Chocolate Jumbles.

½ Cup Butter.   1 Egg.
1 Cup Granulated Sugar.   1 Cup Grated
Chocolate.
1 Cup Brown Sugar.   1 Teaspoon Vanilla.
Flour To Stiffen.
Roll Thin And Bake Quick.

                    Mrs. Gregory.

Hickory-Nut Kisses.

3 Qts Shellbarks (Kernels Picked Out).
1 Lb. Sugar.
Whites Of Five Eggs.
1 Tablespoon Flour.

Beat Whites To Stiff Froth; Add Sugar And Flour Mixed. Add Kernels. Drop Scant Teaspoonfuls On Buttered Paper. Put Paper In Pan And Bake.

                    Mrs. C. W. Bixby

Cinnamon Cakes.

½ Cup Butter.   2 ½ Teaspoons Baking
Powder.
1 Cup Sugar.   1 Tablespoon Cinnamon.
2 Eggs.   Chopped Nuts.
½ Cup Milk.   1 1/4 Cups Flour.

Mix In Order Given And Bake In Buttered Individual Cake Tins. Makes Fifteen Cakes.

                    S. S. Goodwin.

Oat Flake Cookies.

2 Cups Brown Sugar.   ½ Cup Hot
Water.
1 ½ Cup Butter And Lard Mixed. 1 Teaspoon Soda.
2 2 Cups Crushed Oats.   2 Teaspoons
Vanilla.
Flour To Stiffen.
Roll Thin.

                    Mrs. D. H. Eavenson.

Nut Wafers.

1 Lb. Chopped Hickory Nuts.
2 3 Eggs Beaten Separately.
3 Cups Brown Sugar.
4 5 Tablespoons Flour.
2 Tablespoons Butter.
1 Teaspoon Baking Powder.
    Add Nuts Last. Drop In Half Teaspoonfuls
On Well Buttered Pan. Bake In Moderate Oven.

Mrs. C. W. Bixby.

Puffs.

2 Cups Flour.	4 Eggs.
4 Cups Sweet Milk.	Salt.

Dressing For Puffs

1 Cup Sugar.	1 Egg.
Lump Butter.	Vanilla.

Mrs. Keller.

Fruit Jumbles.

1 Cup Butter.	½ Cup Milk.
2 Cups Sugar.	3 Eggs.
3 ½ Cups Flour.	½ Teaspoon Soda.
1 Cup Currants.	½ Nutmeg, Grated.
Bake In Gem Tins.	

Mrs. Gregory.

Drop Cakes.

2 Cups Dark Brown Sugar.	3 Eggs.
1 Cup Butter.	½ Teaspoon Soda.
2 Cups Chopped Raisins.	1 Teaspoon Cinnamon.
½ Cup Chopped Walnuts.	1/2 Teaspoon Cloves.
3 Cups Flour.	2 Tablespoons
Brandy.	

½ Cup Milk.
Drop By Teaspoonfuls On Buttered Tins.

Mrs. H. B. Payne.

Rocks.

1 ½ Cups Brown Sugar.   ½ Glass Sherry Or Brandy.

1 Cup Butter.   3 Eggs.

1 Cup Dates.   1 Lb. English Walnuts,

3 Cups Flour.   1 1/2 Cups Raisins.

1 Teaspoon Soda Dissolved In Warm Water.

Mrs. John Nugent.

Hermits.

2 Cups Brown Sugar.   3 1/2 cups Flour.

1 Cup Butter.   1 Teaspoon Cinnamon.

2 Eggs.   1 Teaspoon Cloves.

1 Cup Sour Milk.   2 Teaspoons Soda.

1 Cup Raisins.

Mrs. Keller.

Macaroons.

Whites Of 4 Eggs, Beaten.   ¾ Cup Flour,

1 Lb. Powdered Sugar.   1 Teaspoon Baking Powder

1 Cup Shellbarks, Chopped Fine.

Macaroons.

Whites Of Three Eggs Beaten Stiff With Small Pinch Soda.

1 Cup Powdered Sugar.

1 Lb. English Walnuts, Chopped.

2 Tablespoons Flour.

3 Vanilla To Taste.

Bake In Moderate Oven.

Mrs. Z. H. Long.

Cocoanut Drops.

Whites Of 2 Eggs Beaten Stiff.   1 Cup Cocoanut.

2 Tablespoons Flour.   1 Cup Sugar

Drop On Buttered Tins. Better Try One, As More Flour May Be Needed.

Miss Esther French.

Orange Puffs.

6 Eggs
1 Pt. Sweet Milk,
1 Tablespoon Melted Butter.   Pinch Salt.
1 Cup Sifted Flour.

Save Whites Of Three Eggs For Sauce. Beat Yolks Till Very Light. Add Butter, Flour, Milk And Whites Of Three Eggs. Bake In Muffin Pans.

Sauce. (Not To Be Cooked).
1 Cup Powdered Sugar.
Juice Of Three Oranges.
Whites Of Three Eggs Well Beaten.

Mrs. George W. Lewis.

Cocoanut Jumbles.

2 Cups Sugar.   2 Eggs.
2 Cups Flour.   1 Grated Cocoanut.
3/4 Cup Butter.

Beat Butter, Sugar And Eggs Very Light.   Add Flour And Cocoanut, Mixing As Little As Possible. Sprinkle With Sugar And Bake A Light Brown.

Miss Elizabeth Loveland.

Boston Cookies.

1 ½ Cups Sugar.   ½ Cup Nuts.
1 Cup Butter.   1 Teaspoon Soda.
5 Eggs.   1 Teaspoons Soda.
2 1/2 Cups Flour.   1 Teaspoon Cloves.
1 Cup Raisins,   2 Teaspoons Cinnamon.
½ Cup Currants,

Chop Fruit And Nuts Mix The Day Before. Roll Thin Adding A Little More More Flour If Necessary.

Mrs. Frederic Corss.

Pepper Nuts.

1 ¾ Lbs Sugar.   1 Teaspoon Soda.

1 Cup Butter.   2 Teaspoons Cream
Tartar

4 Eggs.   1 ½ Lbs. Flour.

1 Cup Sweet Milk.
    Dough Not Too Stiff.

                        Miss Esther French.

Chocolate Puffs.

Whites Of 2 Eggs, Beaten Stiff.
2 Oz. Grated Chocolate, Mixed With2 Tablespoons
Cornstarch.
2 Cups Powdered Sugar.
    Drop From Spoon On Buttered Tins.   Bake In
Moderate oven.

                        Mrs. Wm. Callum.

Oat Meal Cookies.

1 Cup Sugar.   2 ½ Cups Oat Flakes.

1 Tablespoon Butter.   1 Teaspoon Baking Powder.

2 Eggs.   1 Teaspoon Vanilla.

Salt.
    Cream Sugar And Butter And Beat In Eggs. Stir
Baking Powder Through The Oat Flake, Mix And
Drop From Spoon On Well Greased Pan.

                        Mrs. R. A. Hutchison.

Walnut Wafers.

½ Lb. Brown Sugar.   ¼ Teaspoon Baking Powder.

Y₂ Lb. Walnut Meats.   2 Eggs.

3 Even Tablespoons Flour.
    Beat The Whole Eggs Very Light; Add Sugar,
Chopped Nuts, Flour And Baking Powder. Drop
From Teaspoon On Buttered Tins. Bake In Slow
Oven.

                        Miss Elizabeth Loveland.

Ginger Drops.

½ Cup Butter.
1 Cup Molasses.
1 Cup Sugar.
1 Cup Cold Water Or Coffee.
1 Heaping Teaspoon Each Soda, Salt And Pure Ginger.
Flour To Make Batter To Drop From Spoon.
  Drop On Tin And Bake.

Lemon Cookies.

1 Cup Butter.   Grated Rind Of Lemon.
2 Cups Sugar.   1 Qt. Flour.
3 Eggs.
1 Teaspoon Soda In The Juice Of One Lemon.
Mix Soft.

                    Mrs. D. M. Rosser.

Cocoanut Cookies.

½ Cup Butter.   3 Cups Flour.
2 Cups Sugar.   2 Teaspoons Baking
Powder.
2 Eggs.   1/2 Cup Milk,
1Cup Grated Cocoanut.
  Stir Butter And Sugar To Cream. Add Eggs,
Cocoanut, Milk And Flour.   .Roll Thin.
                    Mrs. D. H. Eavenson.

Aunty Hollenback's Shrewsbury Cakes.

1 ½ Lbs. Sugar.
8 Eggs, Minus One-Half The Whites.
1 ½ Lbs. Butter.   4 Tablespoons Cinnamon.
2 Lbs. Flour.   4 Tablespoons
Brandy.
  A Drop Cake.

                    Miss Frances Dorrance.

Small Nut Cakes.

½ Lb. Butter.   4 Eggs.

1 Lb. Sugar.   1 Pint Nuts.
1 Lb. Flour.
Mrs. Grover

Cocoanut Drops.
1 Lb. Grated Cocoanut.
½ Lb. Powdered Sugar.
White Of One Egg.
  Roll All Together, Make Into Little Balls And Bake In Buttered Tins.

                              Mrs. Grover.

Wine Jumbles.
1 Lb. Sugar.   1 Teaspoon Ground Mace.
1 B. Flour.   1 Teaspoon Ground Cinnamon.
¾ Lb. Butter.
6 Eggs.
  Bake In Quick Oven In Shallow Jumble Tins. After Taking From Oven, While Still Warm, Moisten With Cloth Dipped In Wine And Sprinkle Powdered Sugar On Top.

                        Miss Frances Dorrance.

Jumbles.
2 Cups Sugar.   1 Teaspoon Soda.
1 Cup Butter.   2 Teaspoons Cream Tartar.
½ Cup Milk.

                    Miss Jessie Mcfarlane.

Lemon Cheese Cakes.
Juice And Rind Of 4 Lemons.   2 Lbs. Sugar.
½ Lb. Butter.   4 Eggs.
Boil Twenty Minutes. Line Patty Pans With Pastry, Fill With Lemon And Bake.

                        Mrs. Fancourt.

Caraway Seed Cookies.
2 ½ Lbs. Flour.   2 Eggs.
1 Lb. Butter.   ½ Cup Caraway Seeds.

½ Pt. Milk.   1 Teaspoon Salt.
1 ½ Lbs. Sugar.   1 Teaspoon Baking Powder
Mix Well. Roll Thin.

Mrs. H. H. Wells, Jr.

Chocolate Cookies.

3 Eggs.   1 Teaspoon Vanilla.
2 Cups Sugar.   Salt.
½ Cup Butter.   2 Teaspoons Baking
Powder Sifted In Flour.
1 Cup Chocolate.   ½ Cup Milk.
Roll Thin.   Bake In   Quick Oven.

Mrs. R. A. Hutchison.

Wine Drops.

1 Cup Sugar.   1 Teaspoon Soda.
½ Cup Molasses.   Small Teaspoon Cream
Tartar.
½ Cup Sweet Milk.   ½ Teaspoon Each,
Cinnamon, Cloves And Nutmeg.
1/3 Cup Shortening.   ½ Cup Currants Or
Raisins.
  Drop With Spoon On Buttered Tins And Bake In
Hot Oven. May Be Made Without Fruit.

Sugar Cookies.

2/3 Cup Butter.   2 Eggs.
1 ½ Cups Sugar.   2 Teaspoons Of Cream
Tartar.
½ Cup Sweet Milk.   1 Teaspoon Soda.

Mrs. F.W.F.

Cheese Straws.

½ Cup Grated Cheese.   1 Egg.
A Little Pepper.   Flour Enough To Roll Out.
½ Teaspoon Salt.
  Cut Into Narrow Strips And Bake Until Nicely
Brown.

Mrs. Meginess

Icings, Etc.

Lemon Filling.

1 Lemon.	1 Cup Sugar.
2 Eggs.	Butter Size Of Walnut.

Boil Ten Minutes In Double Boiler.

Mrs. Meginess.

Mocha Filling.
1 ½ Cups Powdered Sugar.
1 Teaspoon Vanilla.
2 Dessert Spoons Cocoa.
1 Teaspoon Butter.
Mix All With Cold Coffee So That It Will Spread
Nicely. Put On Layers And Top Of Cake.

Mrs. L,. C. Diggory.

Milk Icing.

1 Cup Sugar.	2 Tablespoons Cream.
5 Tablespoons Milk.	

Boil Sugar And Milk Until It Threads. Add Cream
And Beat Until Cool.

Mrs. J. S. Monks.

Icing No. 1.
Small Piece Butter.
White Of 1 Egg.
1 Cup Powdered Sugar.
Vanilla.

Mix Butter And Sugar. Add Egg And Beat Ten
Minutes. If Too Thick Add Few Drops Of Cream; If
Thin, More Sugar.

J. A. S.

Icing No. 2.

1 Cup Sugar.	2 Tablespoons Cocoa. Vanilla.
3 Tablespoons Cream.	1 Cup Confectioner's Sugar.

Beat Until Very Smooth. Add Five Drops Of Vanilla To

Keep From Cracking.

J. A. S.

Fig Filling.
½ Lb. Raisins.
½ Lb. Dates.
½ Lb. Figs.
   Chop Very Fine, Sweeten And Make Thin Enough
With Water To Spread On Cake.

Mrs. B. R. Tubbs.

Nut Filling.
1 Cup Sour Cream.
1 Cup Chopped Nuts.
1 Cup Sugar.
Boil Seven Minutes.

Mrs. Meginess.

Chocolate Icing.
5 Heaping Tablespoons Grated Chocolate.
1 Egg, Beaten.
1 Cup Sugar.
1 Tablespoon Cream.
Stir All Together And Let Come To Boil.

Mrs. F. L. Olds.

Apple Filling.

1 Cup Sugar.	Juice Of ½ Lemon,
1 Apple, Grated.	White Of 1 Egg.

   Beat All Together Until Like Whipped Cream. To Be
   Eaten Fresh.

Bread, Muffins, Etc.

Graham Bread.

2 ½ Cups Sour Milk.	2 Teaspoons Soda.

½ Cup Molasses.   1 Teaspoon Salt.
4 Cups Graham Flour.
    Let Rise Forty-Five Minutes. Bake Forty-Five
Minutes.

                        Mrs. Keller.

Graham Bread.
2 ½ Cups Hot Liquid (Water Or Milk.
3 Cups Graham Flour, Sifted.
½ Cup Molasses.
1 1/2 Teaspoons Salt.
3 Cups Flour.
1 Tablespoon Shortening.
1 Yeast Cake.
    Makes Two Small Loaves.
                        S. S. Goodwin.

Graham Bread.
1 Pt. Buttermilk Or Sour Milk.   2 Cups Graham
Flour.
½ Cup Sugar.   ½ Cup
Molasses.
1 Cup Flour.   1 Teaspoon Soda.
½ Cup Cornmeal.   1 Teaspoon Salt.
Bake In Oven.

                        Mrs. Murdock.

Boston Brown Bread.
2 Cups Sour Milk.   ½ Cup Molasses.
1 Cup Warm Water.   1 Heaping Teaspoon Soda.
1 Cup Flour.   ½ Teaspoon Salt.
3 Cups Cornmeal.
    Steam Two Hours.

                        Mrs. T. L. Welles.

Entire Wheat Bread.
4 Cups Entire Wheat Flour.
2 Cups Milk.

                                        142

1 Cup Molasses With One Teaspoon Soda Beaten
Into It Until It Foams.
1 Teaspoon Salt.
2 Teaspoons Baking Powder.
   Steam In One Pound Baking Powder Cans One
Hour, Then Brown In Oven.

                              Mrs. Murdock.

Corn Bread.

1 Egg.	1 Cup Flour.
½ Cup Sugar.	2 Teaspoons Baking Powder.
1 Cup Milk.	Pinch Of Salt.
1 ½ Cups Cornmeal.	

   Melt One Tablespoon Lard And Add Last. Bake In
Quick Oven.

                              Mrs. L. C. Darte.

Corn Bread.

1 1Pt. Indian Meal	1 Pt. Milk.
1 Pt. Flour.	2 Eggs.
2 1 Cup Sugar.	2 Teaspoons Baking
Powder	
L/2 Cup Butter.	

                              Mrs. Geo. F. Lee.

Brown Bread.

1 Cup Sour Milk.	1 Egg.
1 Cup Meal,	1 Pt. Milk.
1 Cup Flour.	2 Teaspoons
Baking Powder	
½ Cup Molasses.	

   Steam Three Hours.

                              Mrs. Brewster.

Corn Muffins.

1 Cup Sweet Milk.	Butter Size Of Egg.
½ Cup Sugar (Scant).	1 Egg.
1 Cup Cornmeal.	2 Teaspoons Baking
Powder.	

1 ½ Cups Flour.

Mrs. Geo. H. Ives.

Corn Muffins.

½ Cup Sugar.   2 Eggs.
½ Cup Butter.   2 Heaping Teaspoons Baking
Powder.
½ Cup Cornmeal (Scant).   1 Cup Milk.
Mrs. C. W. Bixby.

Corn Muffins.

½ Cup Butter (Scant).   1 ½ Cups Cornmeal.
½ Cup Sugar.   1 ½ Cups Wheat Flour.
2 Eggs.   2 Small Teaspoons Baking
Powder.
1 Cup Milk.
   If Butter Is Fresh, Add Salt.

Mrs. Von Krug.

Muffins.

½ Cup Sugar.   1 Cup Milk.
1 Tablespoon Butter.   2 Teaspoons Baking
  Powder.
2 Eggs.   Flour To Stiffen.

Mrs. Frane.

Muffins.

1 Pt. Flour.   2 Teaspoons Baking Powder
1 Cup Milk.   Butter Size Of An Egg.
2 Eggs.
   Beat Yolks With Butter. Add Well-Beaten Whites.
Sift Baking Powder With Flour.   Bake In Muffin
Rings.

Mrs. A. Raub.

Muffins.

2 Tablespoons Melted Butter.   3 Cups Flour.
5 Teaspoons Baking Powder.   2 Tablespoons
Sugar.

1 ½ Cups Sweet Milk.   2 Eggs.
Bake In Gem Tins In Hot Oven.

                              Mrs. W. F. Church.

Quick Muffins.
2 Eggs.   1 Teaspoon Salt (Small.)
1 Pt. Sweet Milk.   2 Level   Teaspoons Baking
  Powder.
2 Cups Flour.   1 Tablespoon Melted Butter.
   Beat Eggs Separately. Add Milk And Other
Ingredients Gradually To Yolks. Beat Until Smooth
And Light, Adding Well-Beaten Whites Last. Bake
In Well Greased Muffin Rings On A Griddle Or In
The Oven. Pans Must Be Hot Or Batter Will Run
Under Rings. If Baked On Griddle, Turn To Bake
Both Sides.

                              Mrs. Frederick Corss.

Johnny Cake.
1 Cup Sour Milk.   1 Teaspoon Soda.
½ Cup Molasses   1 ½ Cups Cornmeal.
1 Egg.   ½ Cup Flour.
2 Tablespoons Melted Butter.
Makes One Pan Of Johnny Cake.

                              Mrs. R. B. Vaughn.

Johnny Cake.
1Pt. Milk.   1pt. Cornmeal.
1 Tablespoons Wheat Flour.   Butter Size Of Egg.
2 Eggs, Beaten Separately.
2 Teaspoons Baking Powder.
   Beat Very Hard.

                              Mrs. John Remmell.

Johnny Cake.
1 Egg, Well Beaten.   ½ Cup Sugar And
Molasses Mixed.
1 ½ Cups Buttermilk.   1 Cup Flour.
1 Tablespoon Melted Butter.

1 Teaspoon Soda.

Salt.

Meal Enough To Thicken Like Cake.

Mrs. Gregory.

Johnny Cake.
1 Cup Cornmeal.

1 Teaspoon Salt.

1 Cup Flour.

1 Large Tablespoon Shortening.

1 Cup Sweet Milk.

2 Teaspoons Sugar.

Yolk Of 1 Egg.

2 Teaspoons Baking Powder.

Sift Together Cornmeal. Flour, Baking Powder, Sugar And Salt. Rub In Shortening. Add Milk And Beat Until Smooth. Add Yolk And Beat Again. Bake In Loaf.

Mrs. E. E. Buckman.

Graham Gems.
2 Cups Buttermilk Or Sour Milk.

1 Teaspoon Soda.

1 Tablespoon Melted Lard.

½ Teaspoon Salt.

½ Cup Sugar.

Graham Flour Enough To Make Batter That Will Drop From Spoon. Beat Well And Drop Into Hot, Well-Buttered Gem Irons. Bake Ten Minutes In Hot Oven.

Mrs. J. S. Monks.

Graham Gems.
2 Cups Buttermilk.   ½ Tablespoon Salt.

2 Cups Graham Flour.   1 Tablespoon Molasses.

2 Teaspoons Soda (Small).

Butter Size Of Walnut.

Beat Well.   Bake In Hot Gem Pans In Steady Oven.

Mrs. Abram Goodwin.

Rice Gems.

3 Eggs.	1 Tablespoon Melted Butter,
1 Cup Milk.	1Teaspoon Salt.
1 ½ Cups Flour.	1 Teaspoon Baking Powder,
1 Cup Boiled Rice.	

Beat Eggs Separately. Add Milk, Salt, Butter And Flour To Yolks And Beat Until Smooth. Add Rice And Fold In The Whites Of The Eggs, Beaten Stiff With A Grain Of Salt. Bake Fifteen Minutes In Gem Pans In Hot Oven.

Mrs. James H. Hughes.

Mush Gems.

1 Cup Cornmeal.	2 Tablespoons Melted Butter.
1 Cup Water.	1 Teaspoon Salt.
1 Cup Milk.	1 Teaspoon Baking Powder.
3 Eggs Beaten Separately.	

Heat The Milk And Water Together In A Farina Boiler. Add The Cornmeal Slowly And Cook Ten Minutes. Add Butter And Salt And Let Cool. Add Eggs, First Yolks, Then Whites, And The Baking Powder, And Bake In Muffin ; Ans In Moderate Oven.

Miss Frances Dorrance.

Pop Overs.

1Cup Milk.	1 Egg.
1 Cup Flour.	½Teaspoon Salt.

Put All Ingredients Together In Bowl And Beat Five Minutes With Dover Egg Beater. Bake Twenty-Five Minutes In Hot Oven.

Mrs. C. W. Bixby.

Pop Overs.

2 Eggs.	1 Cup Milk.

2 Tablespoons Sugar.   4 Teaspoons
Baking Powder.
1 Qt. Flour.   Salt.
   Bake In Very Hot Oven.
                         Mrs. W. L. Dean.

Hot Cross Buns.
L Qt. Milk.
½ Lb. Currants.
1 Cup Sugar.
¼ Lb. Lemon Peel, Sliced Thin.
1/2 Cup Melted Butter.
¼ Nutmeg, Grated.
1Yeast Cake.
   Make Sponge With Milk And Yeast Cake And Let
Stand Over Night. In The Morning Add Other
Ingredients And Knead Thoroughly. When Well
Risen Mold Into Oval-Shaped Cakes. Let Rise.
Brush Over With White Of Egg, Make A Cross On
Top And Bake In Quick Oven.
                         Mrs. Fancourt.

Potato Buns.
1 Cup Mashed Potato.   1 Cup Yeast.
1Cup Sugar.
   Let Stand All Night. In The Morning Add:
   3 Eggs.   ½ Cup Melted Lard.
Salt, And Flour Enough To Make A Very Stiff
Dough.

Potato Scones.
2 Tablespoons Butter.   2 Teaspoons Baking Powder.
2 Cups Flour.   1 Teaspoon Salt.
2 Cups Mashed Potatoes.
   Enough Sweet Milk To Make A Dough. Rub The
Butter Into The Flour, Add Potatoes, Salt, Baking
Powder And Milk.   Cut An Inch Thick And Bake In
Quick Oven.
                         Mrs. R. A. Hutchison.

Scotch Scones.

4 Cups Flour.   3 Teaspoons Sugar,
1 Teaspoon Soda.   1 Teaspoon Salt,
1 Teaspoon Cream Tartar.
2 Cups Sweet Milk.
Butter Size Of Egg.
 Roll Out One-Half Inch Thick.   Bake On Griddle.

Mrs. D. M. Rosser.

Tea Biscuit.

1Qt. Flour.
1 Tablespoon Sugar.
3 Teaspoons Baking Powder.
1 Tablespoon Butter Or Lard.
1 Teaspoon Salt.
½ Pt. Sweet Milk.
   Mix Flour, Baking Powder, Salt And Sugar And
Put Twice Through Sieve. Rub In Butter. Bake
Fifteen Minutes.

Mrs. W. L. Stewart.

Rusk.

  Make Sponge With:
  1 Cup Flour.
  1 Cup Sweet Milk Boiled And Cooled.
  1 Cup Yeast.
  1 Cup Sugar.
  Let Rise Over Night.
  In Morning Add:
  ½ Cup Sugar.
1 Egg.
½ Cup Butter.
Use Raisins, If You Like Them.

Mrs. M. A. Van Scoy.

Boston Rolls.

Make A Sponge With:
1 Pt. Sweet Milk, Boiled And Cooled.

3 Tablespoons Sugar And Salt.
1 Penny's Worth Yeast.
Flour To Make Thick Batter.

When Well Risen Add Piece Of Butter Size Of Egg, Stiffen Like Bread And Let Rise Again. Roll Out An Inch Thick, Cut With Cake Cutter, Rub Over With Melted Butter, Turn Double And Bake In Quick Oven.

Miss Jessie Macfarlane.

Waffles.
2 Cups Flour.
1 Tablespoon Baking Powder
1 Tablespoon Sugar.
½ Teaspoon Salt.
Sift Together And Add:
Yolks Of 3 Eggs, Well Beaten.
2 Tablespoons Melted Butter.
1 Cup Sweet Milk.
Whites Of 3 Eggs, Beaten Stiff.

Mrs. Elliott R. Morgan.

Waffles.
¾Cup Melted Butter.
1 Teaspoon Salt.
1 Qt. Milk.
Flour To Make Rather Thick Batter.
2 Heaping Teaspoons Baking Powder.
Beat Hard Ten Or Fifteen Minutes.

Mrs. B. R. Tubbs.

Bread Crackers.
2 Lbs. Bread Dough.
6 Oz. Butter, Size Turkey's Egg.

Work Butter Into Dough With Hands. Roll Out Not Quite One-Half Inch Thick, Cut Out, Prick With Fork, Set To Rise. Bake Slowly, Break Apart And Put In Heater To Dry. Cut Dough Right Size With Cutter Before Baking.

English Muffins.

1Pt. Milk.   4

Scant Cups Flour.

4 Tablespoons Melted Butter.

1 Teaspoon Salt.

½ Cake Compressed Yeast Dissolved In One Cup Water.

   Scald The Milk And Let Cool Until Lukewarm. Add Butter, Yeast, Salt And Flour. Beat Well. Let Rise Until Very Light.   Bake In Rings On Griddle.

Miss Loveland.

Short Cake.

1 Large Saucer Butter.

3 Saucers Flour.

1 Cup Powdered Sugar.

   Mix Well, Turn Out On Bake Board And Work Until It Will Roll Out In Three Cakes One-Half Inch Thick. Grease White Paper, Lay Cakes On Paper In A Pan And Bake Brown In Moderate Oven.

Mrs. D. M. Rosser.

Breakfast Cake.

1 Pt Flour.   1 Cup Milk.

1 Egg.   Salt.

1 Tablespoon Melted Butter.

2 Teaspoons Baking Powder.

Eat Hot With Butter.

Mrs. B. R Tubbs.

Virginia Cake Or Bread.

1 Qt. Sour Milk Or Butter Milk.

2 Tablespoons Sugar.

1 Teaspoon Soda.

1 Pt. Cornmeal.

1 Teaspoon Salt.

3 Eggs.

Bake Three-Quarters Of Hour.

Miss Esther French.

Strawberry Short Cake.
½ Cup Butter.
2 Cups Flour.
2 Teaspoons Baking Powder
Milk Enough To Make Stiff Batter Or Soft Dough.
Bake In Quick Oven. Split In Usual Way.

Mrs. Cooper.

Coffee Bread.
1 Qt. Flour.
1 Cup Sugar.
Powder.
2 Cups Milk. Salt.

2 Eggs.
4 Teaspoons Baking

Bake Fifteen Minutes In Quick Oven.

Mrs. Geo. F. Lee

Preserves

Orange Marmalade.
6 Large Washington Navel Oranges.
3 Lemons.

Score The Fruit Deeply Lengthwise, Then Slice Across Very Thin.
To Each Pound Of Fruit Add Three Pints Of Cold Water And Stand Aside For Twenty-Four Hours. Boil Hard For Three-Quarters Of An Hour And Stand Aside Again For Twenty-Four Hours.

To Each Pound Of Fruit Allow One And One-Quarter Pounds Of Sugar. Boil The Fruit Alone Half An Hour Add Sugar And Boil Until It Will Jell.

Mrs. J. R. Davis.

Orange Marmalade.
5 Lbs. Oranges.

5 Lbs. Sugar.

Peel The Oranges And Put Peels Through Meat Grinder.
Put Peels On To Boil In Cold Water. When They Boil Pour
Off The Water And Repeat The Process Three Or Four
Times. (It Depends Upon How Bitter You Like Your
Marmalade.) Put Pulp Of Oranges Through Grinder, Boil
Until Tender In Hot Water, Put Pulp, Peels And Sugar
Together And Boil Twenty Minutes.
Don't Let It Burn.

Mrs. John Nugent.

Strawberries Preserved In Sun.

5 Lbs Sugar.

1 Large Coffee Cup Water.

Mix And Boil Twenty Minutes. While Boiling Drop In
Three Pounds Large Berries And Boil Five Minutes. Take
The Berries Out Carefully With Skimmer And Arrange On
Platter. Boil Syrup Until Thick, Pour Over Berries And Let
Them Stand In Hot Sun All Day. Stir Occasionally And
Turn In Syrup. At Night Put In Glasses And Cover With
Bran-Died Paper Or Paraffin. This Is A Splendid Way To
Preserve Pineapple, First Shredding It With A Fork.

Miss Dorrance.

Grape Conserve.

5 Lbs. Grapes.	1 Lb. Raisins, Stoned.
4 Lbs. Sugar.	5 Oranges, Peeled And Cut In Dice.

Rind Of Two Oranges.

Remove Skins From Grapes, Boil The Pulp And Strain
Out Seeds. Add Raisins And Grape Skins And Boil Twenty
Minutes. Add Oranges And Sugar And Boil Ten Minutes
More.

Mrs. John Nugent.

Rhubarb Conserve.

4 lbs. Rhubarb.	3 Oranges.
3 1/2 lbs. Sugar.	1 Lb. Seedless Raisins.

Chop All Fine And Cook Until It Jellies.

Mrs. L. C. Diggory.

Green Gooseberry Jam.
1 Lb. Fruit.
¾ Lb. Sugar.
½ Teacup Water.
   Boil Fruit Half Hour. Add Sugar And Boil Until The Proper Thickness,—Twenty Minutes Or More.
                                        Mrs. M. A. Van Scoy.

Brandied Peaches.

4 Lbs. Fruit.	1 Pt. Brandy.
3 Lbs. Sugar.	½ Pt. Water.

   Put Sugar And Water In Preserving Kettle; Peel Peaches And Drop Into Boiling Syrup. Let Them Boil Gently Twenty Minutes, Remove Carefully Into Glasses And Let The Syrup Boil Twenty Minutes Longer. Add The Brandy, And Just As The Boiling Point Is Reached, Pour Over The Peaches. Seal At Once.

Gingered Pears.
1 Pk. Pears.
¼ Lb. Ginger Root Broken In Pieces.
   To Each Pound Of Pears Allow:
1 Bowl Water.
¾ Lb. Sugar.
   Boil Until Clear, Or About Three Hours.
                                        Mrs. C. Bach.

Pickled Cherries.
1 Lb. Sugar To 1 Lb. Cherries.
   Pit Cherries And Let Stand Covered With White Wine Vinegar Twenty-Four Hours. Drain And Put In Bowl With Sugar And Stir Until Sugar Is Dissolved.
Can Without Cooking.
                                        Mrs. M. A. Van Scoy.

Preserved Pineapple.
1 ½ Lbs. Sugar To 1 Lb. Fruit.

Slice The Fruit And Place In An Earthen Jar In Layers, With Sugar Between. Cover Closely And Set On Cellar Floor For Twenty-Four Hours. Stir Several Times During The Day. Can Without Heating. The Sugar Must Be Entirely Dissolved.

Miss Elizabeth Loveland.

Crabapple Jelly.

Cut Choice Apples Into Quarters Without Paring Or Coring. Cover With Water And Boil Until Cooked But Not Much Broken. To Every Pint Of Juice Add One Pound Of Sugar. Take About One-Half Pint Of The Juice And Beat Into It When Cold The White Of One Egg. Pour It Into The Kettle With The Rest And Boil Twenty Minutes, Skimming Carefully.

Miss Frances Dorrance.

Cherry Jam.

1 Bowl Cherries Pitted And Chopped.

1 Bowl Sugar.

Heat Juice And Sugar, Add Cherries And Cook To The Thickness Of Cranberries.

Mrs. M. A. Van Scoy.

Spiced Grapes.

5 Lbs. Brown Sugar.

1 Qt. Vinegar.

7 Lbs. Ripe Concord Grapes.

Ground Cinnamon And Cloves To Taste. Squeeze The Grapes From The Skins, Scald The Pulps Until They Will Pass Through Sieve And Put In Kettle With Vinegar. Boil. Add The Skins And Boil One Hour, Or Longer If You Wish Them Thick. These Quantities Are Right For Spiced Plums.

Miss Frances Dorrance.

Conserve.

3 Lbs. Cherries, Or Currants, Or Plums.

2 Lbs Raisins, Stoned And Steamed Twenty Minutes.

3 Lbs. Sugar.

4 Oranges, Rind Of Two Chopped Fine.
  Cook Twenty Minutes After It Begins To Boil.
                                    S. S. Goodwin.

Conserve.

5 Lbs. Currants.   4 Oranges.
2 ½ Lbs. Raisins.   2 Lbs. Sugar.
  Mash Currants And Boil With Sugar. Put In Chopped
Oranges And Raisins And Boil Twenty Minutes. Can.
                                    Mrs. R. B. Vaughn.

Candied Grape Fruit Peel.

  Cut Peel In Strips Leaving All The White After The Inner
Skin Is Taken Out. Use California Fruit If Possible, As The
Peel Is Thicker And A Deeper Yellow. Soak Over Night In
Weak Salt And Water. Rinse It Thoroughly And Put On To
Boil In Cold Water. Boil For One Hour, Pour Off The Water,
Add Boiling Water And Boil Again, Repeating The Process
Until The Fruit Is Perfectly Tender. If Too Bitter, Pour Water
Off And Use Boiling Water Again. To One Cup Of Peel
Add One Cup Sugar And Half As Much Water. Boil Briskly
Until The Syrup Is All But Gone. Dry Piece By Piece And
Put On Brown Paper. When Cold Roll In White Sugar.
Keep In Air Tight Box.—Glass Or Tin.
                                    Miss Frances Dorrance.

Pickles, Etc.

Tomato Chutney.

50 Large, Ripe Tomatoes.   2 Cups Brown Sugar.
3 Onions, Chopped Fine.   ½ Oz. Whole Allspice.
4 Red Peppers, Cut Fine.   ½ Oz. Whole Cloves.
2 Cups Vinegar.   2 Tablespoons Salt.
  Peel Tomatoes And Cut Up. Mix All Together And
Cook-Slowly Four Or Five Hours, Until Thick. Cool And
Bottle. Seal Tight.
                                    Mrs. Geo. H. Ives.

India Relish.

1 ½ Pecks Green Tomatoes.   L/2 Lb. Whole White Mustard.

½ Peck Onions.   1 Cup Salt.

3 Qts. Vinegar.   ½ Teaspoon Red Pepper.

2 Pounds Brown Sugar.

2 Tablespoons Each Allspice, Cloves, Cinnamon, Ginger And Celery Seed.

    Slice And Chop Onions And Tomatoes. Cover With Salt, Let Stand Over Night. In The Morning Drain, Cover With One Quart Of The Vinegar, Boil Fifteen Minutes. Drain. Put Sugar, Mustard, Pepper And Spices In Remaining Vinegar And Bring To A Boil. Add Tomatoes And Onions And Boil Ten Minutes. Put In Glass Jars While Hot.

                    Mrs. Geo. H. Ives.

French Pickle.

2 Or 3 Carrots.   1 Bunch Celery.

4 Qts. Green Tomatoes.   1 Qt. Small Onions.

1 Head Cauliflower.   6 Peppers, Red And Green.

    Cut Carrots And Celery Into Dice, Chop Tomatoes, Peel Onions, Chop Peppers. Cook Carrots Until Nearly Done. Cook Onions. Separate Cauliflower And Cook Slightly. Let Stand In Weak Brine Twenty-Four Hours. Change Brine And Cook Ten Minutes.

Mustard Paste.

I Tablespoon Turmeric Powder.   3 Teaspoons Ground Mustard.

1 Cup Flour.   5 Cups White Sugar..

    Mix With Water To Form Paste, Pour Into Two And One-Half Quarts Boiling Vinegar. Cook Until Thick, Then Pour Over Pickle And Seal While Hot.

                    Mrs. Geo. W. Lewis.

Chili Sauce.

18 Large Ripe Tomatoes.   6 Onions.

3 Green Peppers.   1 Cup Sugar.

2 ½ Cups Vinegar.   2 Teaspoons Salt.
½ Teaspoon Cloves.
1 Teaspoon Each, Nutmeg, Cinnamon And Allspice.
    Scald And Peel Tomatoes. Cook All Until Tender.
Chop Onions And Peppers.

                              Mrs. C. R. Gregory.

Cucummber Catsup.

Pare Large, Ripe Cucumbers, Remove The Seeds, Grate
And Drain.   To Every Pint Of Grated Pulp Add:
    ½ Pt. Cider Vinegar.
    2 Heaping Tablespoons Grated Horseradish.
¼ Teaspoon Cayenne.
1 Teaspoon Salt.
    Bottle And Seal.

                              Mrs. Franck.

Chili Sauce.

I Peck Tomatoes.   1 Pt. Vinegar.
1 Doz. Onions, Chopped Fine.   1 Cup Sugar.
1 Tablespoon Black Pepper.   ½ Cup Salt.
¼ Teaspoon Cayenne Pepper. 1 Tablespoon Cinnamon.
1 Teaspoon Cloves.
    Boil, But Do Not Strain.

                              Miss Katharine Parsons.

Pickles.

2 Qts. Medium-Sized Onions.
2 Tablespoons Whole Mustard Seed.
2 Qts. Small Cucumbers, Inch In Diameter.
2 Tablespoons Celery Seed.   2 Qts. Vinegar.
1 Teaspoon Turmeric.   1 Large Cup Brown
Sugar.
1 Gill Olive Oil.
    Slice Onions And Cucumbers Crosswise. Sprinkle Salt
Between, And Press In A Colander Over Night. Bring
Vinegar And Sugar To A Boil, Strain And Add Spices And
Oil. Cool And Pour Over Cucumbers And Onions.

                              Mrs. John Nugent.

Favorite Relish.

1 Qt. Cabbage, Chopped Fine.

1 Teaspoon Salt.

1 Qt. Boiled Beets, Chopped Fine.

½ Cup Grated Horseradish,

A Little Black Pepper.　2 Cups Sugar.

　　Cover With Cold Vinegar.　Keep Air Tight.

Pepper Hash.

2 Dozen Peppers.　　　　15 Onions.

3 Tablespoons Salt.　　　½ Cup Sugar.

I Qt. Vinegar.

　　Chop Peppers And Onions, And Pour Over Them
Boiling Water. Let Stand Five Minutes. Drain, Scald Again
And Let Stand Fifteen Minutes. Pour Vinegar, Sugar And
Salt Over Peppers And Onions And Cook Fifteen Minutes.

　　　　　　　　　　　Mrs. T. D. Hutchings.

Spanish Pickle.

8 Qts Cabbage, Chopped.　　8 Qts. Green Tomatoes,
Sliced.

1/2 Cup Salt.　　　　　　1 Doz. Good Sized Onions,
Sliced.

1 Oz. Turmeric.　　　　　1 Oz. Celery Seed.

½ Oz Whole Cloves.　　　1 Oz. Ground Ginger.

½ Lb. White Mustard Seed.　2 1/2 Lbs. Brown Sugar.

4 qts Vinegar.

　　Sprinkle Cabbage And Tomatoes With One-Half Cup
Salt. Let Stand Two Hours. Drain, Add Onions. Put In
Layers In Large Enameled Kettle, Sprinkling Each Layer
With Spices And Sugar. Pour Over Vinegar, Cover And
Boil Fifteen Minutes. Bottle.

　　　　　　　　　　　Mrs. R. P. Brodhead.

Mustard Pickle.

I Qt. Small Cucumbers.　　　　½ Doz. Large
Cucumbers.

1 Qt. Small Onions.　　　1 Qt. Green Tomatoes

3 Green Mangoes, Chopped Fine.

1 Large Cauliflower.

Cut Up Large Cucumbers, Tomatoes And Cauliflower, Add Onions, Small Cucumbers And Mangoes. Let Stand Over Night In A Brine Of Four Quarts Water And One Cup Salt. In The Morning Cook Until Tender, Then Drain. Boil Two Quarts Vinegar And One Cup Sugar Five Minutes. Make A Paste With One Cup Flour, Four Tablespoons Mustard And One Tablespoon Turmeric Mixed With Enough Vinegar To Make Smooth. Add One Tablespoon Celery Seed, And Cook All Together Five Minutes.

Mrs. D. M. Rosser.

Cucumber Pickles.

Select Small Cucumbers. Pour Boiling Water Over Them. Let Stand Until Cool Enough To Handle. Dry On Towel, Pack In Glass Jars One-Third Full; Add One Tablespoon Salt, A Few Bay Leaves, And Repeat Until Jar Is Full. Pour Over Scalding Vinegar Sweetened. Add A Few Cloves And Cinnamon.   Seal. They Can Be Used In Two Weeks.

Mrs. J. D. Flanagan.

Chili Sauce.

1 Peck Ripe Tomatoes, Peeled.

5 Sweet Peppers And 10 Onions Chopped Fine.

1 Cup Sugar.

1 Qt. Vinegar.

½ Cup Salt (Small).

1 Tablespoon Each Of Ginger, Cloves, Allspice And Cinnamon.

Mix All Together And Cook Slowly Two Hours Or Until Thick Enough To Suit.

Mrs. S. E. Leacock.

Beverages

Strawberry And Raspberry Vinegar.

3 Lbs. Ripe Berries.
2 Oz. Citric Acid.
1 Qt. Spring Water.

Dissolve Acid In Water, Pour Over Berries And Stand Twenty-Four Hours. Drain, Strain And Add To Liquor Its Own Weight In Sugar. Boil Five Minutes In Porcelain Kettle.   Cool, Cork Lightly Four Days, Then Seal Tight.

Mrs. John Nugent.

Spanish Chocolate.

1 Qt. Milk.	1 Cake French Chocolate.
Yolks 2 Eggs.	1 Teaspoon Vanilla.

Melt Chocolate And Pour Into Boiling Milk. Whip Eggs To Froth. While Beating Pour In Chocolate A Spoonful At A Time. Add Vanilla. Serve Very Hot With Whipped Cream On Top Of Each Cup.

Miss Frances Dorrance.

Grape Juice.

Cover Grapes With Water And Cook Until Soft. Put In Bag And Drain. Heat Juice, Add Sugar To Taste. Do Not Let Boil.   Bottle While Hot.

Mrs. B. R. Tubbs.

Lemonade For Thirty People.
1 Qt. Lemon Juice.
2 Qts Sugar.
6 Qts. Water.

Add Oranges And Pineapples. Takes 2 Doz. Good Lemons.

Mrs. H. H. Welles, Jr.

Candies, Etc.

Peanut Brittle.
¼ Cup Peanuts.
1/3 Cup Sugar.

Cook Sugar In Iron Sauce Pan Until Liquid. Don't Let It Bubble Or It Will Burn. Add Chopped Peanuts And Pour On Large Inverted Pan Which Has Been Heated And Greased. Roll Out Very Thin With Greased Rolling Pin. Cut In Small Squares And When Cool Turn Upside Down And Hit With Handle Of Knife.   It Will Break Easily.

Fruit Candy.

4 Lbs. Sugar.   1 Lb. Figs.
2 Cups Water.   1 ½ Lbs Dates.
3 Lbs English Walnuts.
2 Heaping Tablespoons Grated Chocolate.
Boil As For Fudge.   Beat Hard When Done.

Mrs. M. A. Van Scoy.

Chocolate Fudge.

2 Cups Sugar.   1 Teaspoon Vanilla.
1 Cup Milk.   Butter Size Walnut.
2 Squares Baker's Chocolate.

Molasses Candy.

2 Cups Molasses.   Butter Size Of Walnut.
1 Cup Sugar.   1 Tablespoon Vinegar.
    Boil Twenty Minutes, Stirring All The Time. Just Before Taking From Fire Add One Teaspoon Soda.

Mrs. B. R. Tubbs.

Chocolate Chew.

1 Lb. Brown Sugar.   2 Tablespoons Molasses.
½ Cup Milk.   Butter Size Of Egg.
¼ Lb. Chocolate.   1 Teaspoon Vanilla.
    Boil Until Hard When Dropped In Water.

Mrs. Von Krug.

Chocolate Fudge.

2 Cups Sugar.   Large Piece Butter.
¼ Cake Chocolate.   Vanilla.
1 Cup Water.

Miscellaneous

Cure For Felons In Six Hours.
1 Tablespoon Dry White Lead.
1 Tablespoon Turpentine.
1 Tablespoon Lard.
1 Tablespoon Sweet Oil.

Simmer On Stove In A Porcelain Dish, Stirring With A Pine Stick Until Of A Light Brown Color. Then Add Tablespoon Flour. Apply Hot.

C. L. T.

To Store Eggs.
5 Gallons Water.
1 Pint Salt.
1 Lb. Lime, Fresh, Unslacked.

Slack Lime With A Little Hot Water In A Stone Jar. Add The Water. Stir Frequently During The Day. Next Morning A Light, Flaky Scum Will Have Formed Over The Top. If This Is Too Thick And Hard A Crust, Add More Water. Add Salt, And When Dissolved, Put In The Eggs.

Miss Frances Dorrance.

To Wash Flannels.
Place Flannels To Soak In Pail Of Water At 100 Degrees Fahrenheit, In Which Ivory Soap Has Been Boiled. Cover Tight And Soak For One Hour. To 6 Qts. Of Water Add 1/3 Cake Ivory Soap.
1 ½ Tablespoons Household Ammonia.
½ Teaspoon Powdered Borax.

Wash Out By Drawing Through The Hand. Do Not Rub. Ring Out Twice In Luke Warm Water And Run Through Wringer. Hang Clothes Lengthwise To Dry. Iron While Damp, Stretch Into Right Shape. Iron Should Not Be Too Hot.

Mrs. J. Ford Dorrance.

Fernban Liniment.

1 Gal. Vinegar.   4 Oz. Oil Organum.

4 Oz. Sugar Of Lead.   4 Oz. Turpentine.

I Oz. Tinct. Iodine.   1 Oz. Spirits Camphor.

2 Oz. Oil Vitrol, Last.

     Fine For Sprains.

C. L. T.

Weights And Measures.

4 Teaspoonfuls, Liquid, Equals 1 Tablespoonful.

3 Teaspoonfuls, Dry. Materials, Equals 1 Tablespoonful.

4 Tablespoonfuls, Liquid, Equals ½ Gill, Or ¼ Cup.

16 Tablespoonfuls, Liquid, Equals 1 Cup Or 1/2 Pint.

12 Tablespoonfuls, Dry Material, Equals ½ Pint.

1 Cup, Liquid, Equals 1/2 Pint.

4 Cups, Liquid, Equals 1 Quart.

4 Cups Flour, Equals 1 Quart Or 1 Pound.

2 Cups Granulated Sugar Equals 1 Pound.

1 Cup Butter Equals ½ Pound.

1 Round Tablepoonful Butter Equals 1 Ounce.

1 Heaping Tablespoonful Butter Equals 2 Ounces, Or ¼ Cup.

1 Heaping Tablespoonful Sugar Equals 1 Ounce.

1 Pinch Of Salt Or Spice Is About 1 Saltspoonful.

Washing Fluid.

1 Box Banner Lye.

2 Oz. Salts Of Tartar.

2 Oz. Sal Ammoniac.

     Dissolve Each Separately Then Put Together.

C. L. T.

Hard Soap.

Dissolve One Box Banner Lye In 3 Pints Of Soft Cold Water.

Heat 5 Lbs. Clean Grease.

1 Handful Borax.

½ Cup Ammonia.

     Put All Together, Stirring Constantly. Then Put In A

Warm Place For 24 Hours. Cut Into Squares And Dry For
Use.

C. L. T.

Baking Powder.

16 Oz. Cornstarch.

8 Oz. Bicarbonate Soda.

5 Oz. Tartaric Acid.

Mix Thoroughly By Putting Through A Sieve Several
Times.   Put In Tight Tin Cans.

Miss Esther French.

Corn.

To Add One Pint Of Milk To Water In Which 1 Dozen
Ears Of Corn Are Boiled Adds To The Flavor Of The Corn.

J. A. S.

To Boil Mush For Frying.

1 Qt. Water.	Butter Size Of Egg.
1 Pt. Milk.	Thicken With Cornmeal.
1 Teaspoon Of Salt.	

Boil Twenty Minutes. When Cold, Fry.

J. A. S.

To Keep Cider Sweet.

26 Gals, Cider.

½ Oz. Salicylic Acid.

1 Oz Gelatin Dissolved In Cold Water.

C. L. T.

French Mustard.

2 ½ Tablespoons Mustard.	1 Egg.
1 Tablespoon Sugar.	1 Cup Vinegar.

Mix Mustard And Sugar Until Smooth, Add Egg, Th?N
Vinegar Gradually, And Cook Until Thick. When Done
Add A Small Piece Of Butter.

Mrs. Albert E. Miller.

Yeast.

165

1 Small Handful Hops.	½ Cup Salt,
1 Qt. Water.	1 Cup Sugar.
4 Large Potatoes.	1 Cup Yeast.

Boil Hop Water, Grated Potatoes, Sugar And Salt Together Until Thick, Then Add Potatoes.

Additional Recipes

Sour Cherries Preserved In Sun.

Wash Cherries, Drain Thoroughly And Pit. To One Pound Cherries Add One Pound Sugar. Let Them Heat Through Slowly Until Sugar Is Dissolved, Then Boil Five Minutes, Skimming Carefully. Dip Out On Large Plates And Set In A Hot Sut For Twelve Hours. They Must Have Twelve Hours Of Sun If It Takes Two Or Three Days To Get It. Cover With Mosquito Netting And Draw A Chalk Line Around Whatever They Are In To Keep Away Ants. When Fruit Is Clear They Are Done And Can Be Put In Jars. Do Not Heat Again.

Miss Elizabeth Loveland.

Celery Soup.
| 1 Pt. Sliced Celery. | 1 Pt. Hot Cream. |
| 1 Tablespoon Rice. | Salt And Pepper To Taste. |

Boil Celery And Rice Together And Put Through Sieve. There Should Be A Quart Of The Mixture After It Goes Through Sieve. Add Cream And Seasoning.

Mrs. R. P. Brodhead

Potato Soup.
4 Large Potatoes Cut In Quarters.	1 Pt. Hot Cream.
1 Tablespoon Chopped Parsley.	1 Small Onion.
1 Bay Leaf.	Salt And
Pepper.	

Boil Potatoes Ten Minutes, Pour Off Water, And Boil Again In One Quart Of Boiling Water Until Fully Dissolved. Put Through Sieve And Add Other Ingredients.

Miss Elizabeth Loveland.

Cream Tomato Soup.

1 Qt. Strained Tomatoes.   Pinch Of Soda Size Of Pea.
1 Cup Hot Cream.   Salt And Pepper.
   Serve With Toast Croutons

Mrs. Wells.

Chicken Noodle Soup.

Beat One Egg, Add As Much Flour As Egg Will Take Up, Season With Salt And Roll As Thin As Possible. Hang To Dry, Roll Up And Slice Very Thin. Drop Into Boiling Soup Made From The Neck, Wings And Bones Of Chicken. Add A Little Parsley With The Noodles.

Mrs. Wells.

Clam Chowder (For Small Family).

6 Large Potatoes Cut In Dice.   Butter Size Of Egg.
1 Teaspoon Allspice.   1 Cup Milk Or
Cream,
1 Doz. Clams.   Salt And Pepper,
1 Tablespoon Flour.

Put Allspice In Bag And Boil With Potatoes. When Potatoes Are Done Take Out Bag And Add Clams Cut In Pieces. Do Not Boil After Adding The Cream.

Mrs. Wells.

Cheese Dumplings.

1 Pt. Milk.   ½ Teaspoon Salt.
2 Tablespoons Butter.   ½ Saltspoon White Pepper.
6 Tablespoons Flour.   ½ Cup Grated Cheese.

Make Thick Cream Dressing With First Five Ingredients And When It Begins To Boil Add Cheese.

For The Dumplings Take:
2 Eggs, Beaten Very Light.   ½ Cup Grated
Cheese.
8 Tablespoons Milk.   ½ Teaspoon Salt.
Shake Of Red Pepper.

Flour Enough To Make Batter That Will Keep Shape Of Spoon.

Drop The Dumplings From Spoon Into Hot Cream Diess-Ing, Sprinkle Grated Cheese Over The Pan And Bake In Quick Oven Twenty Minutes.   Serve At Once.

Miss Elizabeth Loveland.

Apple Snow.

Pare And Stew Eight Tart, Juicy Apples. Strain, Sweeten And Flavor With Lemon And, When Cool, Break In The Whites Of Two Eggs. Beat Briskly. Serve With Whipped Cream Or Boiled Custard.

Mrs. Wells.

Chocolate Pudding.

4 Oz. Sweet Chocolate.	2 Cups Sugar.
1 Qt. Milk.	1 Cup Stoned Raisins.
1 Pt. Bread Crumbs.	1 Cup Blanched Almonds.
4 Eggs, Well Beaten.	Nutmeg.
1 Cup Butter.	

Boil Chocolate In Milk, Pour Over Bread Crumbs And Let Stand One Hour. Add Other Ingredients And Steam Two Hours.

Mrs. Wells.

Nut Cake.

1/2 Cup Butter.	2 1/2 Cups Flour.
1 Cup Sugar.	1 ½ Teaspoons Baking Powder.
3 Eggs.	1/2 Cup Milk.
1 Cup Chopped Nuts.	

Make Into A Firm Batter.

Mrs. Wells.

Appendix A

KINGSTON BUSINESS DIRECTORY – Purden 1902

PROPRIETOR	BUSINESS/LOCATION
Andrews, Wm.	Bakery and Confectionary/ W. Market
Aston, E. R.	General Merchandise/ Main St.
Atkinson, J.J.	Barber Shop and Pool/ Wyoming Ave.
Bach, C.	Merchant, Tailor and Furnisher/ 23 W. Market
Balanis, John	Confectionary/Center St.
Beck, Harry	Restaurant, Wines, Liquors, and Cigars/ Market and Page Streets
Benedik, T.	Saloon/Center St.
Boone, C.W. & J.P.	Real Estate/ W. Market
Bound, H. C.	Barber/16 W. Market
Boyd, S. D.	Confectionary and Restaurant/ 8 Wyoming Avenue and 9 W. Market
Boyer, W. H.	Groceries, Provisions, Etc./ 206 E. Market
Breisch, W. H.	Druggist/ W. Market
Brown, F. L.	Jeweler/ W. Market
Burton, J. A	Groceries, Dry Goods, etc./ 36-38 Wyoming Avenue
Carle, Ira	Justice of the Peace/ Wyoming Avenue
Carr, G. W.	Florist/232 Maple St
Case, James	Confectionary/18 E. Market St
Central Penn Tel. and Supply Co., Exchange	Chestnut nr. Market St.
Cloauser, Dr.	College
Cobleigh, B. J.	Physician/ W. Market
Collins, M. H.	Barber/ Main St
Coolbaugh, E. H.	Dentist/ Wyoming Ave.
Cross, Frederick	Physician/ N. Maple
Covert, M.M.	Confectionary, Ice Cream, Restaurant
Daley, T.	Confectionary/W. Market St

PROPRIETOR	BUSINESS/LOCATION
Deposit and Savings Bank. Capital $50,000; surplus $35,000.	Daniel Edwards, Pres.; T. L. Newell, vice pres.; E. M. Rosser, cashier./ Cor. Chestnut and Market St.
Donahue, J. P., prop'r	Central Hotel /Kingston Corners
Doron W. E. & Son	Undertakers/18 W. Market
Dougherty Bros.	Bottlers/ Cor. Wyoming Avenue and E. Market St
Dougherty, T. P.	Restaurant, Wines, Liquors, etc./
Drochak, Alex.	Saloon/ Main St
Edwards & Co.	General Merchandise, Hardware, Etc/. Cor. Market and Page
Evans & Son.	Druggists/ cor. Market and Page
Exchange Hotel	Wyoming Avenue
Farrell, F. A.	Physician/ W. Market St
Frantz, Bros.	/Market/ W. Market St
Gallagher, C. J.	Tailor/ W. Market St
Garshan, M.	Gardner/ Main St
Gittins, S.	Wallpaper, Painting, Paints, Oils, Etc.
Gray, Albert W.	Barber Shop/ Wyoming Avenue
Hammond, J. P.	Confectionary//15 Main St
Hendershot, F. A. & N. M.	Bicycle Repairing/ Wyoming Ave. nr. Market St
Himelsteib, I.	Confectionary and Variety Goods/ Main St
Hopkins, David. asst. sup.	Met Life Ins. Co./ Edwards Building
Hoskien, John	Saloon/ Main St
Hotel Polski, Peter Passa, prop'r	Main and D.L. & W. R.R.
Howe, James	Jeweler/ Main St
Hutchison, R. A.	Groceries/ W. Market St
Hyndman & Garney	Dry Good, Notions, and Groceries/ 40-42 Wyoming Avenue
Jacobs, E. B.	Blacksmith/ cor. Market and Rutter Ave.
Johnson, H. F. & Son.	Plumbing/15-17 E. Market St
Jones, Isaac	Groceries, Shoes, Etc./ W. Market St/

PROPRIETOR	BUSINESS/LOCATION
Kingston Coal Co.	opp. D.L. & W. depot
Kingston Feed Mill Millard & Scureman prop'rs.	Flour, Feed, Grain, Hay, Straw, Salt, Etc.// above D.L. & W. depot
Kingston House, J. B. Wandell, prop'r.	opp. D.L. & W. depot
Kingston Lumber Co.,	Office/ Pringle
Kingston Market, H. L. Bicks, prop'r.	Kingston Corners
Kosztecsky, Mrs.	Midwife/ Center St
Kraft, Fred	Bakery/13 Wyost.ming Avenue
Kundracka, Chas.	Saloon// Center
Lake, D. H.	Physician/ S. Maple
Lavis, William	Barber / at Kingston House
Law, John	Grocer/ Main St
Lee, Tom	Laundry/111 W. Market St.
Levine, L.	Cigars and Candles/ Main cor. Center
Stephens, Stephen	Restaurant/ Center St
Talbot, Wm. H.	Barber/ W. Market St
Townend, C. W.	Livery/ W. Market opp. P.O.
Turpin, F. C.	Grocer/ Wyoming Avenue
Van Horn, W.M.	Blacksmith/207 E. Market
Walsh, M. F.	Wines and Liquors/ Main St
Weiss, A. L.	Shoemaker/ Kingston Corners
Welsh, R.J.	Saloon/ Main St
Wilkes-Barre Record	west side office/ W. Market St
Wilkes-Barre Times	west side office/ Edwards bldg.
Wilcox, C. R.	Brick manufacturer/31 S. Maple St
Wright, Frank E.	Manufacturer of carriagesWyoming Avenue nr. Market St
Wyoming college of Business, W.L. Dean, A.M. principal	Market St
Wyoming Seminary, Rev. L/L. Sprague, M.A. President	Market and College St
Youdziawicz, Adam	Saloon and Grocery/ Center St

Appendix B

RECIPE Contributors: Selected Data from the
1910 United States Federal Census[24]

Contributor's name, address and number of recipes.	Born In U.S.	Age 1907	Head of Household/ Relationship /Age/ Occupation	Children –at Home Name/ Age	Ser-vant
Bach, Mrs. C. (Sarah) 219 College (Sprague) Ave. Kingston, PA 7 recipes	Yes	57	Christian/H/57/ Tailor	Mary – 21	
Benner, Mrs. (Bessie) 341 Wyoming Avenue Kingston, PA 1 recipe	Yes	31	Issac/E/41 Proprietor Plumping Co.		
Bixby, Mrs. C. W. (Anne S.) Wilkes-Barre, PA 16 recipes	Yes	53	Charles W./H/ (52) /Cemetery Secretary	Elenor – 22 Evard - 20	Yes
Brewster, Mrs. (Mary) 252 College (Sprague) Avenue Kingston, PA 8 recipes	Yes	58	William/S/ 30/Lawyer		Yes
Brodhead, Mrs. R. P. (Fannie) 131 Maple Street (Avenue) Kingston, PA 3 recipes	Yes	45	Robert P. /H/46/ Owner Concrete Works	William-16 Elimra-14 Mary-11 Francis-10 James-7 Charles-1	Yes
Buckman, Mrs. E.E. (Bertha) 335 Wyoming Avenue Kingston, PA 4 recipes	Yes	41	Elmer/H/ 45/Assistant Bank Cashier	Helen-12 Alice-11 Henry-4	
Butler, Mrs. Pierce (Mary) 52 Butler St. Dorranceton, PA 2 recipes	Yes	52	Pierce/H/52/ Auditor	Mary Jr.-8 Charlotte Breadier-27 Foster Daughter	

Contributor's name, address and number of recipes.	Born In U.S.	Age 1907	Head of Household/ Relationship /Age/ Occupation	Children –at Home Name/ Age	Ser- vant
Church, Mrs. W. F. (Anna) 63 Pringle Street Kingston, PA 3 recipes	Yes	55	William/H/61/ Druggist	H. Kenneth -29 Mary L.-28 Elizabeth-2 5 Charles-24 Frederick-2 1	
Cooper, Mrs. (Sofia) 73 Pringle Street Kingston, PA 2 recipes	Yes	59	Sofia/S/59	Franklin-28 Hannah-17	
Corss, Mrs. Frederick (Martha) 214 Maple Street (Avenue) Kingston, PA 3 recipes	Yes	58	Frederick /H/ 65/ Physician		Yes
Croll, Mrs. James S. (Margaret) 458 S. Franklin Street Wilkes-Barre, PA 2 recipes	Yes	37	James/H/39/ Departmnt store buyer	Elsie-3 Joseph-8 Jane-6	Yes
Darte, Mrs. L.C. (Josephine) 243 Maple Street 3 recipes	Yes	43	Luther/H/ 65/Own Income	Morley-5	Yes
Dean, W.L. (Mary G.) 361 Wyoming Avenue Kingston, PA 8 recipes	Yes	50	Willis L./H/50/ Professor- Wyoming Seminary		Yes
Diggory, Mrs. L. C. (Laura) 390 Walnut (Mercer) Ave. Kingston, PA 4 recipes	Yes	44	Laura/S/44	Benjamin-2 0 Book- keeper	
Dorrance, J. Ford (Elizabeth D.) Dorranceton, PA 2 recipes	Yes	52	J. Ford /H/56	Susan-30 Sturgis-25 Charles-25	Yes

Contributor's name, address and number of recipes.	Born In U.S.	Age 1907	Head of Household/ Relationship /Age/ Occupation	Children –at Home Name/ Age	Ser- vant
Dorrance, Miss Frances 1 Dorrance Farm Dorranceton, PA 19 recipes	Yes	29	Benjamin/F/ 60/Farmer		Yes
Eavenson, Mrs. D. H. (Elisa J.) 342 Ridge Avenue 6 recipes	Yes	55	David/H/55 Locomotive Engineer	Norris -22 Bertha-23 Anna -16	
Ellis, Mrs. H.G. (Jesse) 385 Maple Street (Avenue) Kingston, PA 2 recipes	Yes	34	Horace/H/34/ Coal company payroll clerk		
Faulds, Mrs. W. H. (Ella M.) 467 Wyoming Avenue Kingston, PA 3 recipes	Yes	54	William/H/ 57/ Physician		Yes
Flanagan, Mrs. J.D. (Julia D.) 265 Maple Avenue Kingston, PA 4 recipes	Yes	42	George/H/ 53/ Bank Cashier	Emily-9	Yes
Mrs. W. L. Foster (Ellen) 13 York Avenue West Pittston, PA 1 recipe	Yes	41	William/H/44/ Assistant Cashier	Donald-16 Elsie-14 Catharine-8	Yes
Franck, Mrs. (Hannah) 73 Pringle Street Kingston, PA 6 recipes	Yes	70	Sophia/SIS/ 59		
Frane, Mrs. (Elizabeth) 86 Thomas Avenue Dorranceton, PA 1 recipe	Yes	37	William/H/36/ Clerk, Post Office	Hazel-12 Meta-8 Wilma-1	

Contributor's name, address and number of recipes.	Born In U.S.	Age 1907	Head of Household/ Relationship /Age/ Occupation	Children –at Home Name/ Age	Ser- vant
Frantz, Mrs. F. W. (Julia E.) 175 Maple Street (Avenue) Kingston, PA 3 recipes	Yes	31	Fred/H/32/ Owner Building Materials	John-1	
French, Miss Esther 1399 Wyoming Avenue Forty Fort, PA 15 recipes	Yes	27	Harry/F/70/ Farmer		
Gage, Mrs. E. G. (Margaret) 220 Exeter Street West Pittston, PA 2 recipes	Yes	37	Erastus/H/ 39/ Insurance Agent	Anna-14 Charles-7	
Goodwin, Miss Helen 48 Pringle Street Kingston, PA 3 recipes	Yes	31	Frank/F/60		
Goodwin, Mrs. Abram (Emma) 1 recipe	Yes	62			
Goodwin, Mrs. S.S. (Sophia) 285 Maple Street 6 recipes	Yes	34	William/H/34/ Lawyer	Willard-7	
Gregory, Mrs. (Elizabeth) Kingston, PA 5 recipes	Wales	31	William/H/42/ Chief of Police	Lottie-7 Rosina-5 Emily-3 George-24	
Mrs. Grover (Anna) 256 Maple Street (Avenue) Kingston, PA 2 recipes	Yes	49	Millard/H/56/	Nellie-30 Alfred-24	
Nellie Grover 256 Maple Street (Avenue) Kingston, PA 3 recipes	Yes	30	Millard/F/ 56/		

Contributor's name, address and number of recipes.	Born In U.S.	Age 1907	Head of Household/ Relationship /Age/ Occupation	Children –at Home Name/ Age	Servant
Hessel, Mrs. Philip (Helen) 427 Rutter Avenue Kingston, PA 3 recipes	Yes	27	Philip/H/36/ Real Estate Agent	Harold-5	Yes
Hilbert, Mrs. Wesley (Hattie) 152 Bennett Street Dorranceton, PA 2 recipes	Yes	28	Wesley/H/ 36/ Carpenter	Lila-11 Robert-5 Wesley-3 Fannie-1	
Hoyt, Miss Augusta 243 Maple Street (Avenue) Kingston, PA 6 recipes	Yes	50	Edward/B/48/ Lawyer	Patience-11	Yes
Hughes, Mrs. James H. (Emma) 465 Wyoming Avenue Kingston, PA 6 recipes	Yes	45	James/H/47/ Mining engineer	3	Yes
Hutchinson, Mrs. R.A. (Francis) 258 Chestnut Avenue Kingston, PA 3 recipes	Yes	55	Robert/H/ 55/Salesman	Archibald-16 Donald-15 James-11	
Ives, Mrs. George H. (Alice) 534 Wyoming Avenue Dorranceton, PA	No/ Eng- land	46	George/H/ 51/ Music Dealer	Marion-17 Martha-15 Alice -12 Helen-13	Yes
Jenkins, Mrs. John E. (Katherine) 322 Maple Avenue Kingston, PA 2 recipes	Yes	43	John/H/44 Lawyer	Mitchell-11 Hugh-7	
Mrs. Keller (Magaret) 326 College (Sprague) Kingston, PA 4 recipes	No/ Scot- land	56	Zach/H/57 Construction Foreman	Ralph-27	

Contributor's name, address and number of recipes.	Born In U.S.	Age 1907	Head of Household/ Relationship /Age/ Occupation	Children –at Home Name/ Age	Ser-vant
Lake, Mrs. D. H. (Mary) 137 Maple Street (Avenue) Kingston, PA 3 recipes	Yes	37	David/H/43 / Physician	Louise-16 Margaret-1 3	Yes
Lawley, Miss (Isabelle and/or Anna) 292 Rutter Avenue 3 recipes	No/ Can-ada	36, 33	Richard/F/ 75/ Farmer		
Lee, Mrs. George F. (Phebe) 504 Wyoming Avenue Dorranceton, PA 5 recipes	Yes	33	George/H/ 35/ Lumber merchant	John-12 Abbie-10 Phebe Jr.--8	Yes
Lewis, Mrs. George (Amanda) 185 College (Sprague) Ave. 4 recipes	Yes	51	George/H/ 58/ Laborer, Kingston Borough	Andrew-28 Ruth-14	
Loveland, Miss Elizabeth 134 Maple Avenue Kingston, PA 25 recipes	Yes	43	Self/ Real estate income		
MacFarlane, Miss Jesse 363 Rutter Avenue 22 recipes	Yes	44	Thomas/F/ 72		Yes
Mrs. Markle (Mary) 60 Goodwin Avenue Dorranceton, PA 1 recipe	Yes	31	Charles/H/36/ Coachman	Ruth-11 Loretta-10 Hazel-6 Mabeld-7 Frances-2	
Marvin, Mrs. M.E. (Bertha) 19 Main Street Kingston, PA 1 recipe	Yes	33	M. E./H/34 Physician		

Contributor's name, address and number of recipes.	Born In U.S.	Age 1907	Head of Household/ Relationship /Age/ Occupation	Children –at Home Name/ Age	Ser- vant
Meginess, Mrs. (Lavinia) 23 Carle Street 9 recipes	Yes	44	David/H/51 Coal miner	Gertrude-24	
Miller, Mrs. Albert E. (Jessie) 255 Wyoming Avenue Kingston, PA 5 recipes	No/ Can-ada	38	Albert/H/ 38/ Undertaker		Yes
Monks, Mrs. J.S. (Susan) 383 Maple Avenue 2 recipes	Yes	37	Miles/F/72 Contractor		
Morgan, Mrs. Elliott (Maggie) 239 Maple Avenue Kingston, PA 1 recipe	Yes	52	Elliot/H/52 Secretary, Kingston Coal Co.	Lua-18 Ruth-12	
Murdock, Mrs. (Lucy) 150 Maple Street (Avenue) Kingston, PA 3 recipes	Yes	40	Leonard/H/43/ Methodist Minister	Harriet-14	
Newitt, Mrs. (Janette) 312 Ridge Street Kingston, PA 2 recipes	Yes	45	Joseph/H/ 43 Boiler Inspector Railroaad	Warren-19 George-14 Amy-10	
Nugent, Mrs. John (Fidelia) 321 Wyoming Avenue Kingston, PA 1 recipe	Yes	45	John/H/47/ Secretary Coal Company	Louisa-25 Harold-23	Yes
Olds, Mrs. F.L. (Mary) 71 James Street Dorranceton, PA 3 recipes	Yes	37	Frederick/H/55 Architect	Carolyn-11 Kate-9 Sara-4	Yes

Contributor's name, address and number of recipes.	Born In U.S.	Age 1907	Head of Household/ Relationship /Age/ Occupation	Children –at Home Name/ Age	Ser-vant
Miss Nellie Parry 402 Wyoming Avenue Kingston, PA 3 recipes	Yes	37	John/F/65 Superintendent of Mines		
Parsons, Miss Katharine 188 S. Franklin Street Wilkes-Barre, PA 4 recipes	Yes	38	Self/Teacher		Yes
Payne, Mrs. H. B. (Gescela) 306 Maple Avenue Kingston, PA 5 recipes	Yes	33	Hubert or Hubbard/H/36 Lawyer	Hubert-3	Yes
Mrs. T. L. Phillips (Isabella) 240 Maple St. (Avenue) Kingston, PA	Yes	57	Thomas/H/61/ Clerk	Mat-24 Blanche-22 Courtney-16	Yes
Raub, Miss (Miria and/ or Anna) 398 Wyoming Avenue Kingston, PA 8 recipes	Yes	50 54	Anna/S/54		
Rosser, Mrs. M. D. (Mary) 167 Maple Street (Avenue) Kingston, PA 3 recipes	Yes	31	David/H/37 Building Contractor	Charles-7 Robert-1	
Scureman, Mrs. Mark A. (Blanche) 340 Maple Avenue Kingston, PA 3 recipes	Yes	34	Mark/H/36 Insurance Agent	Margaret-9 Harry-7 Arvilla-1	
Mrs. George Shoemaker (Anna) Wyoming Avenue Forty Fort PA	Yes	61	George/H/ 62/ Real Estate		Yes

Contributor's name, address and number of recipes.	Born In U.S.	Age 1907	Head of Household/ Relationship /Age/ Occupation	Children –at Home Name/ Age	Ser-vant
Smythe, Mrs. H.C. (Sara) 69 James Street Dorranceton, PA	Yes	34	Hugh/H/37 Lawyer	Abram-2	Yes
Snow, Mrs. (Edith) 105 Kusckka (sp) Street 1 recipe		17	Oscar/ Teamster		
Sperling, Mrs. J.G. (Margaret) 458 Wyoming Avenue Kingston, PA 2 recipes	No-Ger-many	48	John/H/73/ Physcian	Edith-25 Frederick-24 Grace-18	
Tubbs, Mrs. B. R. (Carrie) 46 Wyoming Avenue 20 recipes	Yes	56	Benjamin/H/57/ Druggist	Henry-26 Clara-22 Robert-22	Yes
Van Scoy, M. A. (Mary A.) 341 Wyoming Avenue 8 recipes	Yes	62	Issac/S/41 Proprietor Plumping Co.	Issac-41	Yes
Vaughn, Mrs. R.B. (Rilla) 246 Chestnut Street 9 recipes	Yes	42	Robert/H/ 47/Agent Machinery Co.	Helen-18 Florence-16 Ralph-13	
von Krug, Mrs. (Jennie) Wyoming Avenue Wyoming, PA 5 recipes	Yes	51	Ferdinand/H/ 57/ Clergyman	Carl-27 Annie-15	Yes
Welles, Mrs. H. H. (Anna) 385 River Street Forty Fort, PA 3 recipes	Mrs. H. H. Welles is Theodore L. Welles's deceased mother. Perhaps someone like Mrs. Welles' daughter Charlotte or her daughter-in-law Catherine submitted the recipes in her honor.				
Welles, T. L. (Catherine) 385 River Street Forty Fort, PA 5 recipes	Yes	42	Theodore/H/44 Civil Engineer	Ted Jr.-15 John-10 Carolyn-8	Yes

Endnotes

[1] Reichl, R 2003 Modern Food Library Series Introduction Random House, <http://www.randomhouse.com/ modernlibrary/seriesfooddet1.html> (accessed 27 September 2007).

[2] The 1910 Federal Census population count was 6,649 persons.

[3] The 1950 Federal Census population count was 21,096 persons.

[4] Kraut, Alan M. The Huddled Masses: The immigrant in American Society 1880 - 1921. Second Edition. Harland Davidson Inc.:   Wheeling, IL 2001. P. 70

[5] Dillingham Commission (1907-1910). http://ocp.hul.harvard.edu/immigration/dilligham.html (Accessed 19 February 2012).

[6] Sources: http://bitsandpieces1.blogspot.com/2007/07/1907-one hundred-years-ago.html, http://www.historyorb.com/events/date/1907, : Information Please: 1907 http://www.infoplease.com/year/1907.html#ixzz1fnUuxVqw

[7] History of Luzerne County. http://www.luzernecounty.org/living/history_of_luzerne_county (Accessed 3 February 2012).

[8] U. S. Bureau of the Census. Thirteenth Census of the United States: 1910 Volume 3: Population – Pennsylvania. Table I. Composition and Characteristics of the Population for the State and the Counties. P. 580

[9] U. S. Bureau of the Census. Thirteenth Census of the United States: 1910 Volume 3: Population – Pennsylvania. Table I. Population of Minor Civil Divisions: 1910, 1900, 1890. P. 545.

[10] U. S. Bureau of the Census. Thirteenth Census of the United States: 1910 Volume 3: Population – Pennsylvania. Table IV. Composition and Characteristics of the Population for Places of 2,500 to 10,000. P. 597.

[11] The Austria-Hungary Empire of 1910 included present day Austria, Hungary, Bosnia and Herzegovina, Croatia, the Czech Republic, Slovakia, Slovenia, large parts of Serbia and Romania and smaller parts of Italy, Montenegro, Poland and Ukraine.

[12] U. S. Bureau of the Census. Thirteenth Census of the United States: 1910 Volume 3: Population – Pennsylvania. Table I. Composition and Characteristics of the Population for the State and the Counties. P. 580

[13] The Courthouse Gang on Yahoo. 1907 and 1908 Wilkes-Barre Record Almanac(s) Record of Local Events for 1906 and 1907 http://freepages.genealogy.rootsweb.ancestry.com/~wbalmanacs/almanacs.htm. (Accessed 29 February 2012). The Wilkes-Barre Record newspaper was published from 1881 to 1972. In addition to a daily newspaper an almanac was also published. Many of the Almanac from 1885 thru the 1960's have transcribed by members of The Courthouse Gang on Yahoo.

[14] Gibson, Campbell. Population of the 100 Largest Urban Places: 1910. http://www.census.gov/population/www/documentation/twps0027/tab14.txt (Accessed 23 Feb 2012.

[15] Phillips, Edward, D. History of Luzerne County, unpublished manuscript, Luzerne County Historical Society.

[16] Brewster, W. A. History of the Certified Township of Kingston, PA 1769 to 1920. Kingston Borough School District (1930). P. 438 – 443.

[17] Phillips, Edward, D. History of Luzerne County, unpublished manuscript, Luzerne County Historical Society.

[18] Martin, Elizabeth. "Wyoming Valley Women's Club Makes Giving Fashionable" Independent NEPA, 16 December 2009. http://independentnepa.com/component/content/article/556. (Accessed 4 March 2012).

[19] Nativism is prejudice against immigrants in favor of the native born members of a particular society. It is often associated with racism in that the targets of nativism typically belong to a different ethnic group than the perpetrators (About.com).

[20] Roller, Anne R. "Wilkes-Barre: An Anthracite Town" The Survey (1 February 1926): 534-538.

[21] Roller, Anne R. "Wilkes-Barre: An Anthracite Town," The Survey (1 February 1926): 534-538.

[22] History of Luzerne County. http://www.luzernecounty.org/living/history_of_luzerne_county (Accessed 3 February 2012).

[23] Adapted from the Watkins Woolen Mill State Historic Site, Missouri Department of Natural Resources, Division of State Parks.

[24] Most of the information in this table was taken from the U. S. Bureau of the Census. Thirteenth Census of the United States Census, 1910. In a few cases, when a household record could not be found in the 1910 Census, information was taken from the 1900 Census.